CAR SMARTS

Hot Tips for the Car Crazy

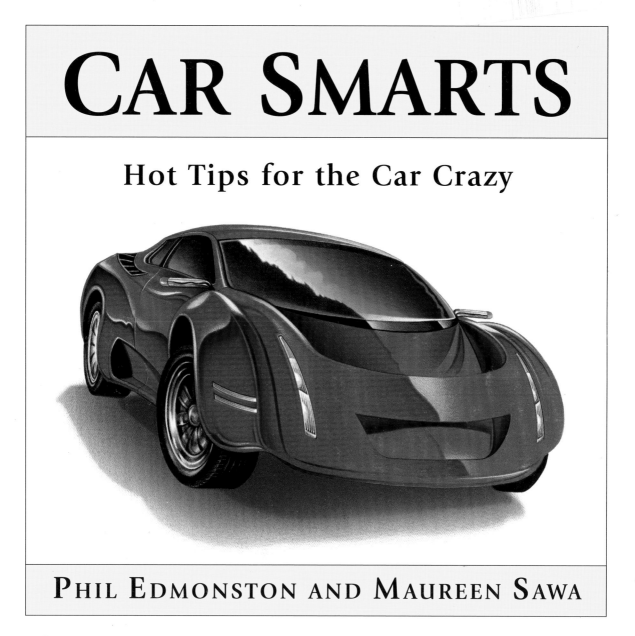

PHIL EDMONSTON AND MAUREEN SAWA

ILLUSTRATED BY GORDON SAUVÉ

Tundra Books

St. Brigid School
730 Citadel Way NW
Calgary, Alberta

Text copyright © 2004 by Phil Edmonston and Maureen Sawa
Illustrations copyright © 2004 by Gordon Sauvé

Published in Canada by Tundra Books,
481 University Avenue, Toronto, Ontario M5G 2E9

Published in the United States by Tundra Books of Northern New York,
P.O. Box 1030, Plattsburgh, New York 12901

Library of Congress Control Number: 2003106149

All rights reserved. The use of any part of this publication reproduced,
transmitted in any form or by any means, electronic, mechanical, photocopying,
recording, or otherwise, or stored in a retrieval system, without the prior written
consent of the publisher – or, in case of photocopying or other reprographic
copying, a licence from the Canadian Copyright Licensing Agency – is an
infringement of the copyright law.

National Library of Canada Cataloguing in Publication

Edmonston, Louis-Philippe, 1944 –
    Car smarts : hot tips for the car crazy / Phil Edmonston, Maureen Sawa ;
illustrated by Gordon Sauvé.

Includes index.
ISBN 0-88776-646-3

    1. Automobiles – Juvenile literature. I. Sawa, Maureen II. Sauvé, Gordon
III. Title.

TL147.E352004   j629.222   C2003-903050-4

We acknowledge the financial support of the Government of Canada through
the Book Publishing Industry Development Program (BPIDP) and that of the
Government of Ontario through the Ontario Media Development Corporation's
Ontario Book Initiative. We further acknowledge the support of the Canada
Council for the Arts and the Ontario Arts Council for our publishing program.

Design: Kong Njo
Additional illustration: Rick Jacobson and Mor

Photo credits: The images on pages 1, 13, 25, 35, 37, 49, 52, 57, and 61 are courtesy
of the Special Collections Department of the Hamilton (Ontario) Public Library;
the image on page 10 is courtesy of the Glenbow Archives (NA-1790-1).

Printed and bound in Canada

1 2 3 4 5 6   09 08 07 06 05 04

CONTENTS

Acknowledgments   iv

Chapter 1: **Automotive History 101**   1

Chapter 2: **From Combustion to Computers:**

       How a Car Works   13

Chapter 3: **Car Design: From Function to Style**   25

Chapter 4: **What Makes a Good Car?**   37

Chapter 5: **Car Ownership: Making the Grade**   49

Chapter 6: **Cars of Tomorrow – Today**   61

Where to Look   73

Glossary   75

Index   76

ACKNOWLEDGMENTS

We wish to thank our most amazing editor, Janice Weaver, for steering us in all the right directions, and our designer, Kong Njo, for his skill and artistry in creating such a wonderful layout. Our illustrator, Gordon Sauvé, is truly gifted. We are indebted also to the inspiration of our publisher, Kathy Lowinger, whose vision and innate ability to see an opportunity brought us all together in the first place. We are very grateful, as well, to all the people at Tundra, who have been so very supportive and encouraging throughout the process of creating this book.

We also would like to express our appreciation to Margaret Houghton, of the Special Collections Department of the Hamilton Public Library, for her detective work in locating archival images and information. Special thanks also to Daniel Malstrom for his time and expertise.

Finally, we thank our "back-seat driver," Jake Sawa, whose unique perspective and keen insights ensured that we stayed on track.

1

AUTOMOTIVE HISTORY 101

The invention of the automobile is widely considered the single most important development in the history of transportation since the discovery of the wheel. Cars have increased personal mobility and permitted people to live farther and farther from their workplaces, leading to the formation of suburbs and the increase in urban sprawl. Cars and trucks bring goods and services to shopping malls and even right to our front doors. We judge others and ourselves by what kinds of cars we drive. Special memories – of family trips, first dates, and friends – are often made in cars. And although we're sometimes frustrated by how much time and money our cars devour, we can't imagine life without them.

The automobile as we know it was not invented in a single day by one individual. Instead, it was the result of an evolution in technology that took place worldwide over centuries. Many inventors dreamed of building self-propelled machines, and plans for motor vehicles were actually drawn up by both Leonardo da Vinci and Isaac Newton!

The Automotive Family Tree

Although Karl Benz is credited with building (in 1885) the prototype of the modern car, the first self-propelled vehicle was actually invented more than one hundred years earlier, by Nicolas Cugnot in 1769. But unlike the "Benz model," which used an internal combustion engine, Cugnot's car, and most of the machines designed during that period, was steam-propelled.

Cugnot, a French military engineer, developed his steam-powered vehicle as a gun carriage to help the French army move its artillery pieces in and around the city of Paris. Although it was tested on the grounds of the Paris Arsenal, the three-wheeled machine, which had its engine and boiler in the front, was never used in an actual battle. Because it was capable of attaining speeds of only about four miles (6 kilometers) an hour, it was far too heavy and slow to be of practical use.

Nevertheless, Cugnot's machine was significant. In using steam to produce the energy to power his vehicle, the Frenchman was drawing on knowledge that can actually be traced back to the time of the ancient Egyptians. The physicist Denis Papin (1647–1712) was an important pioneer in this field. Fascinated by gases and vacuums, he invented the pressure cooker and devised a simple steam pump to provide power for fountains. Eventually, he designed an engine that was supposed to use steam to raise a piston inside a cylinder, creating a vacuum as it rose. Although Papin never managed to make an engine that really worked, this principle is the basis on which all steam engines operate. Steam engines have been used to power ships and trains for many years, and even today, thermal power plants generate electricity by using steam power.

The Chinese constructed the world's first permanent road system around 1000 B.C., but the Romans are history's master road-builders. Throughout their vast empire, they constructed 53,000 miles (85,000 kilometers) of roads, primarily for military use. The most famous of these was the Appian Way, built in 312 B.C. This ancient highway was so well built that parts of the road are still in use today.

THE WHEEL OF FORTUNE

The wheel and the concept of continuous rotation date from more than five thousand years ago to Mesopotamia (a region of modern-day Iraq). The wheel would eventually make it easier for people to transport goods from one place to another, accelerating the growth of trade and exchange.

We know that the first road vehicles were two-wheeled carts, with crude disks fashioned from stone serving as the wheels. Used by the Sumerians (*c.* 3000 B.C.), these simple wagons were the precursors of the chariot, which was made famous by the Greeks and Romans. By the first century A.D., the wheel had spread throughout the Mediterranean and into northern Europe and eastern Asia. Despite the many other advancements of ancient civilizations in the Americas, however, the wheel was not introduced there until the Europeans arrived in the sixteenth century.

Life without wheels is even more unthinkable than life without cars! Not only does the wheel make possible all forms of transportation, but many different machines – elevators, cranes, pulleys, and so on – use wheels to operate. Truly, the wheel is one of our greatest inventions.

How Steam Makes Power

Steam is made when water is heated to high temperatures and changes into a gas. It's a vapor that moves so fast it wants to take up more space and will try to escape from the container in which it's being heated. When you heat water in a pot with a lid, for example, the pressure from the steam that is eventually generated will build until it actually raises the lid and creates a means of escape. When enough steam has been released, the pressure lowers and the lid falls back in place with a rattle.

Steam engines operate on this same principle. Fuels like coal and oil are burnt in a huge furnace to heat water and make steam. The engine then converts this heat energy into mechanical energy by allowing the steam to alternately expand and cool. This process moves the engine's pistons, which turn a crankshaft that is connected to wheels by a chain or a driveshaft. That's how the wheels begin to turn.

The difficulty with early steam engines was that they could quickly overheat and become dangerous. They required a great amount of coal to raise the steam, and the cost of all that fuel was prohibitively high. But in the late 1700s, James Watt, a

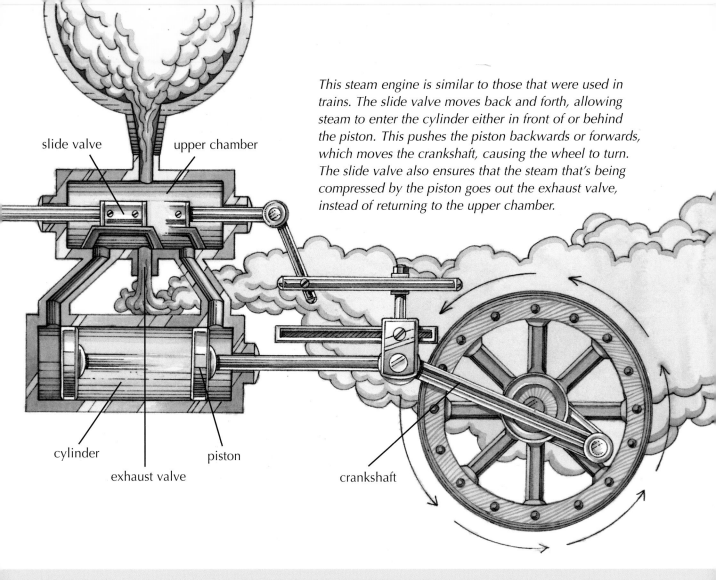

This steam engine is similar to those that were used in trains. The slide valve moves back and forth, allowing steam to enter the cylinder either in front of or behind the piston. This pushes the piston backwards or forwards, which moves the crankshaft, causing the wheel to turn. The slide valve also ensures that the steam that's being compressed by the piston goes out the exhaust valve, instead of returning to the upper chamber.

slide valve

upper chamber

cylinder

exhaust valve

piston

crankshaft

JAMES WATT AND "HORSEPOWER"

Watt was a very canny Scotsman, and he understood the value of getting a patent for his new method of "lessening the consumption of steam and fuel in fire engines." This was an advancement that paved the way for the invention of the first steam-powered railroad locomotive in the early nineteenth century, and because Watt was clever enough to obtain a patent, he and his company, Boulton & Watt, had a virtual monopoly over the production of steam engines for twenty-five years.

How did Watt put his patent to use? He charged his customers a premium for using his steam engines, which he rationalized by comparing his machine to a horse. Watt calculated that a horse was capable of pulling 180 pounds (80 kilograms), on average, and whenever he made a machine, he described its power in relation to a horse's. So a twenty-horsepower engine was capable of pulling 3,600 pounds (1,600 kilograms), or doing the work of twenty horses. To calculate his fee, Watt worked out how much each company saved by using his machine rather than a team of horses. The company then had to pay him one-third of that figure every year for the next twenty-five years.

Scottish instrument maker, made the historic improvements that moved the steam engine forward. He designed a working prototype for a steam vehicle in 1784, and soon many other inventors, buoyed by his success, tried developing engines that would be suitable for transport. By 1804, there were steam locomotives that could haul heavy loads and also transport people. Soon the idea of railroads began to catch on in France, Germany, and North America. Rapid improvements in the refinement of steam engines quickly followed, and in no time, long-distance transport and travel was cheap and accessible, changing the way people lived. Towns were built close to rail lines, and by the late 1800s, it was possible to cross the United States or Canada from the Atlantic to the Pacific coasts by rail.

Yet despite the success of steam power, many scientists and inventors were convinced that even more effective ways of running an engine could be developed. People began searching for a more compact and convenient alternative for powering pumps, factory machines, and transport vehicles, and through tinkering and experimentation, the modern internal combustion engine was eventually born.

The "Infernal" Combustion Engine

Like the car itself, the internal combustion engine wasn't created by any one person. Instead, improvements by several different inventors led to a machine that was lighter, more compact, and more easily controllable than the steam engine.

In Switzerland, Isaac de Rivaz designed many successful steam-run cars toward the end of the eighteenth century. He is generally credited with building the first internal combustion engine in 1807. In these kinds of engines, the fuel is burned inside the engine itself, not in a separate boiler, as happens with a steam engine. De Rivaz's engine was gas-driven and used a mixture of hydrogen and oxygen to generate energy. He used this engine to power a car, which was probably the first vehicle to run on an internal combustion engine.

Jean Joseph Etienne Lenoir of Belgium also experimented with these engines, and unlike Rivaz, he was able to market them successfully. Lenoir's engines were more popular because

A patent gives its owner the exclusive right to make, use, or sell her invention for a period of years. Most countries of the world have patent systems, although the terms will vary from place to place.

they used gas for fuel, instead of Rivaz's hydrogen-and-oxygen mixture. In 1862, Lenoir built a two-stroke engine with a single cylinder and electric ignition that could go almost two miles (3 kilometers) an hour. A year later, he put a variation of the same engine into a "horseless carriage" and attained a speed of three miles (5 kilometers) an hour. By 1865, there were actually five hundred of his engines in use in Paris alone.

After Germany's Nicolaus Otto read of Lenoir's two-stroke, gas-driven internal combustion engine, he began working on his own model in a workshop in Deutz, near Cologne. In 1863, he found a way of improving Lenoir's engine to make it a practical power source, and in 1876, he created the first four-stroke internal combustion engine, a real alternative to the steam engine and the most efficient gas engine produced up to that time. Otto patented his invention in 1877, calling it the Otto Cycle Engine. Unfortunately, his patent was invalidated in 1886 when it was discovered that another inventor, Alphonse Beau de Rochas, had already described the engine in a privately published pamphlet.

Only the very rich could afford to purchase cars in the early days of automobile manufacturing in Europe. In fact, Gottlieb Daimler initially believed that Europe would never see more than about five thousand cars. Why? That's how many chauffeurs there were, and no self-respecting gentleman would drive his own carriage!

THE DIESEL ENGINE

Rudolf Diesel was born in Paris in 1858. He designed many heat engines, including a solar-powered air engine. In 1893, he published a paper describing an internal combustion engine that would use the heat from compression rather than a spark to ignite the fuel. In 1894, he filed for a patent for this new invention, dubbed the diesel engine.

Diesel operated his first successful engine in 1897. With it, he demonstrated that air could be compressed so much that heat would be created, raising the temperature to levels that would far exceed the ignition temperature of the fuel. Although never as popular as gasoline engines, the diesel engine has remained a viable alternative for many drivers throughout the world because it burns less fuel and has fewer parts to service.

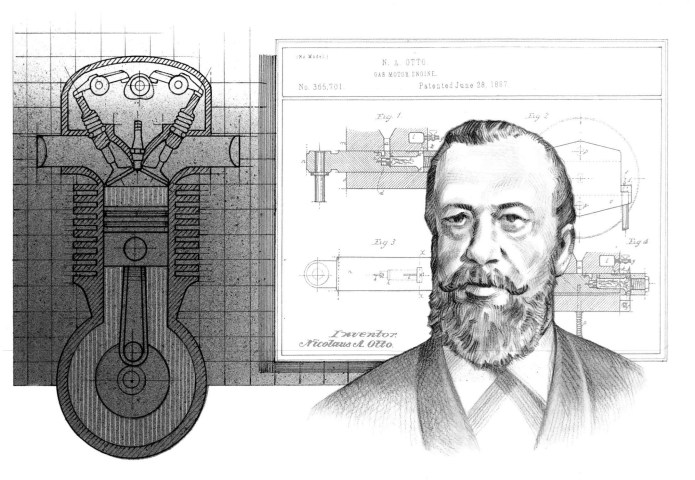

Nicolaus Otto with one of the patents he was granted for a gas-powered engine. His prototypes are still the model for the internal combustion engines we use today.

Nevertheless, Otto's compressed-charge engine marked the beginning of an era and was the foundation of the modern engine. Still, it was not originally intended for transport. Instead, it was meant to replace steam engines in powering factories. And it had one great drawback that made it impractical for use in vehicles – the engine had to be connected to a gas supply for refueling. The solution was an engine that would run on liquid fuels that would create gas in the combustion chamber. At the time, oil was used mainly for lighting and cooking. But with the advent of Otto's engine, some inventors began to see the possibilities of using it as a fuel for engines.

It was a colleague of Otto's, a German engineer named Gottlieb Daimler, who carried out much of the development work on the gasoline-fueled internal combustion engine. His improvements made it smaller, more lightweight, and faster to run. In 1882, Daimler left Otto's company and set up his own business with a partner, William Maybach. Three years later, he and Maybach fitted their engine to a bicycle and created the prototype of the present-day motorcycle. Daimler then came up with the idea of adding an internal combustion engine to a bicycle that had been stabilized with side wheels, producing one of the first "motor vehicles." A year later, in 1886, he fitted one of his engines to a horse-carriage and created the first four-wheeled motor car in history. Amazingly, in that same year, another German engineer, Karl Benz, patented a similar engine – one with an electric ignition, differential gears, and water-cooling – and fitted it to a tricycle. Soon, Benz also applied this technology to four-wheeled carriages, creating the first of the modern automobiles.

Benz's car, however, was not an immediate commercial success. Seven years passed, in fact, before the vehicle caught on. With twelve hundred units built, the 1894 Benz Velo became the first mass-produced car sold to the general public.

Unlike Benz, Daimler focused his attention only on his engines. He sold them to a French company, Panhard et Levassor, which built bodies for them. This company was the first to regard the car as a machine in its own right. The bodies produced by Panhard et Levassor did not simply copy the design of horse-drawn carriages, but instead provided innovations such as a hood over the engine, a metal chassis, a clutch, and brake and accelerator pads. In 1891, Panhard et Levassor moved the engine from the back of the car to the front, away from the debris thrown up by the wheels. In effect, the company gave the automobile a layout and structure that laid the foundation for a newly emerging American automotive industry.

The Car in North America

In North America, there wasn't quite as much tinkering with steam and internal combustion engines. Here, automobiles trace their heritage more to the bicycle industry of the 1890s. In fact, most of the early car pioneers in America were men who built, sold, and serviced bicycles.

Charles and Frank Duryea were two such bicycle makers. Charles spotted a gasoline engine at the 1886 Ohio State Fair and became convinced that an engine-driven carriage could be a reality. The two brothers designed and built the car together, showing off their invention on the streets of Springfield,

Cyclists can be thanked for generating government road-building projects in North America. In the early 1890s, a national "good roads" movement was sponsored by American cycling groups, and this led to the creation, in 1902, of what later became known as the Bureau of Public Roads. This agency was established to gather national, state, and local cooperation for the permanent improvement of public highways. In 1967, it became the Federal Highway Administration. It continues to lobby for better roads to this day, supported by the Canadian Automobile Association and the American Automobile Association.

In rural Pennsylvania at the turn of the last century, a group of farmers formed the Farmers' Anti-Automobile Society to set down some rules for car owners. Automobiles traveling at night had to send up a Roman candle (a type of flare) every mile, wait ten minutes for the road to clear, and then proceed (with caution) while blowing the horn. If a driver saw horses coming, he had to pull over to the side of the road, stop, and wait for them to pass!

Massachusetts, on September 22, 1893. They were the first in the country to manufacture and sell cars that were powered by an internal combustion engine. By 1896, they had built thirteen of these.

Bicycle manufactures also provided the engineering, parts, and facilities for the fledgling automobile trade. In fact, the local bicycle shop was where most North Americans bought their cars, until the first automobile showroom opened in New York City in 1900.

But eventually car manufacturing was taken out of the hands of the smaller-scale bicycle makers and became an industry in its own right. Although Henry Ford is commonly referred to as the father of this industry in North America, it was actually Ransom Eli Olds who first mass-produced cars to be sold to the public. He introduced the assembly-line concept and established a factory in Detroit, Michigan, to manufacture several prototype automobiles. Detroit was the natural choice, since it was already home to a number of firms that made carriages, bicycles, and boat engines. It would eventually become the world's largest auto-making center. Unfortunately, Olds's factory burned down in 1901, after just fourteen years of production, and only one prototype – the Curved Dash Olds, a single-cylinder buggy with a curved dash – survived. This car, also called the Oldsmobile Gas Buggy, sold more units than any other American car of its time. In 1908, the Oldsmobile Company was joined by Buick, and together they soon formed the General Motors Group.

As cars slowly took their place on the roads alongside horses, public response varied from excitement to fear. There were laws that required motorists to stop completely while buggies, surreys (small carriages), and freight wagons dragged by. Speed limits as low as two and three miles (3 to 5 kilometers) per hour were imposed by a few communities. In smaller towns, in particular, marshals and other law officials lay in wait for unsuspecting drivers, timing them by stopwatch. Lawmen were authorized to shoot at tires or stretch chains or wire across the road to stop those who endangered public safety by daring to "hurtle" along at more than a snail's pace.

Despite all these efforts to control the spread of automobiles, people just had to have them. Henry Ford recognized that

In 1907, the town of Glencoe, Illinois, built humps in the streets to discourage speeding. Three years earlier, townspeople had stretched a steel cable across the road to stop the "devil wagons."

Ransom Olds's ill-fated Curved Dash Olds hardly seemed designed for the unpaved streets that were everywhere in early 1900s North America.

THE FIRST LEMON?

The early Model T had so many quirks and defects that it's unlikely liability lawyers would pass it today. Because the car lacked a fuel pump, gasoline flow to the engine was controlled strictly by gravity. This system worked fine until drivers encountered long, steep hills, where the car would always stall. Ford, made aware of this problem, simply put out the word that drivers should back up long inclines instead of approaching them head on – and many owners did just that without any lawsuits or nation-wide recall campaigns!

The popularity of the Model T put pressure on governments to become more directly involved in road development, particularly in rural areas. Car manufacturers in North America aggressively marketed their vehicles to farm families, who generally lived a great distance from the nearest town. The movement to improve highway conditions soon became known as the push to "get farmers out of the mud."

there was a need for a car that was affordable and accessible to the general public, and he understood that the way to do this was to make each one exactly like all the others with identical parts. He opened his first car plant – also in Detroit – in 1903. On the Ford assembly line, a rope pulled a line of car chassis along a track manned by fifty workers, each fixing his own allotted part to each chassis as it moved by. As the cars rolled down the line, a worker would repeat the same operation on each one, over and over again. With this method, the assembly time for a chassis dropped from twelve hours to one and a half.

The first car that Ford's assembly line produced, called the Model T, cost less than other cars but was still sturdy and practical. It had a four-cylinder, twenty-horsepower engine, and it reached a top speed of forty miles (65 kilometers) per hour. From 1915 to 1925, it came in only one color: black. This was because black paint dried faster than other colors, making it possible for the Ford plant to produce more cars in a shorter period of time. And the more cars the company could produce, the more affordable they would become – although the $850 starting price was the equivalent of a teacher's annual salary! By 1927, the price of a Model T had dropped to $260.

Popularly known as the "Tin Lizzie" (because the body was made of lightweight sheet steel, like tin, and Lizzie was a name commonly given to horses at that time), the Model T was a major hit. Ford sold 15 million from 1908 to 1927, the only years it was in production. Though the car could seat just two people, it sold more than any other type of car at that time. Because it was both affordable and practical, it was truly the first "people's car," with farmers, factory workers, schoolteachers, and many other Americans making the switch from horses or trains as a result. But Henry Ford thought of cars as appliances or commodities, much like refrigerators or washing machines, so he didn't believe in tinkering with design or trying to improve the Model T to keep it popular. General Motors, meanwhile, introduced the concept of an annual model change, and soon the Model T was losing out to its competitors. By 1927, production was stopped.

It was in the 1920s that the so-called Big Three automakers emerged. Ford was soon competing with the General Motors Corporation (an amalgam of companies, including Chevrolet, Cadillac, Pontiac, Oakland, Oldsmobile, and Buick) and Walter P. Chrysler's Company (founded in 1925). Through recessions, strikes, times of peace and times of war, these three companies have continued to exercise tremendous influence over the world's automobile industry. But consolidation of the industry is accelerating. Today, the eight leading manufacturing groups are BMW, DaimlerChrysler (which includes Mercedes-Benz, Mitsubishi, Hyundai, and Maserati), General Motors (which now includes Daewoo, Isuzu, Saab, and parts of Lada, Subaru, Suzuki, and Toyota), Honda, Ford (which includes Jaguar, Rover, and Volvo, plus parts of Mazda), Toyota, Renault (includes Nissan), and Volkswagen (includes Audi, Porsche, and Rolls-Royce). This merging of automakers has been so successful, in fact, that Toyota now threatens to permanently replace DaimlerChrysler as the third member of the Big Three.

From power steam to gasoline, the history of the automobile has taken many twists and turns. Later on in this book, we'll see how car manufacturing is likely to develop in the future. But now, let's take a closer look at what's inside cars today.

The phrase "people's car" was first used in the 1930s to describe the original Volkswagen Beetle. (The word *Volkswagen*, in fact, is German for "people's car.") The Beetle was designed by Ferdinand Porsche to meet the need for a compact, durable car that people could easily afford. Eventually, the Beetle became the most popular car ever built, and car manufacturers have been trying to design the next "people's car" ever since.

CHAPTER 2

FROM COMBUSTION TO COMPUTERS: HOW A CAR WORKS

Cars can be beautiful and mysterious. They are styled to look fast even when they're standing still, and everything that makes them go is hidden away underneath sheet metal and fiberglass. But a car is a complicated piece of machinery. Like a symphony orchestra, it depends on all its parts – its diverse operating systems – performing together in harmony. And when you put the key in the ignition, you are like a conductor raising his baton.

When they are trying to ensure that a car is completely "in tune," auto mechanics typically look first to four main areas: the engine, the transmission, the wheels, and the chassis. There are a number of other key systems – including braking, cooling, electrical, exhaust, heating, and fuel and intake – that also need to be working together before a car can perform at its best, but the first four are the most important. With that in mind, let's learn a little bit about what it takes to make a good car work well. We'll start with the car's heart – its engine.

The Engine

Turning a key in the ignition triggers a complex sequence of events that gets your car moving. First, the battery completes an electrical circuit, and that activates the electronic control unit, the fuel pump, and the fuel injectors. At the same time,

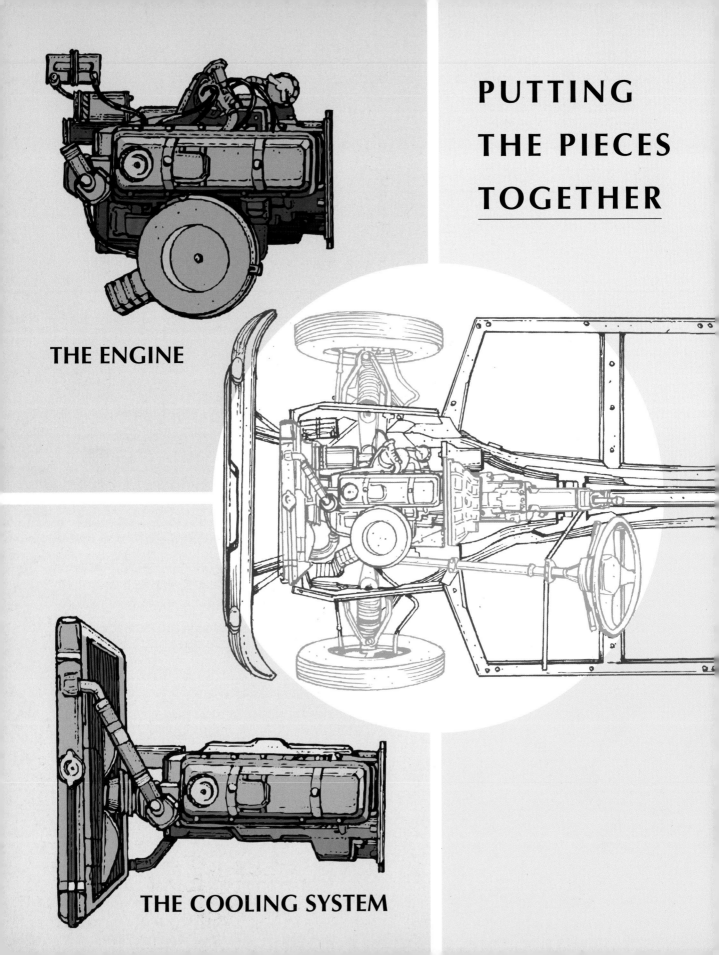

PUTTING THE PIECES TOGETHER

THE ENGINE

THE COOLING SYSTEM

This illustration shows how the major systems of the car fit together. In the pages that follow, we'll learn more about the components that make up each of these systems.

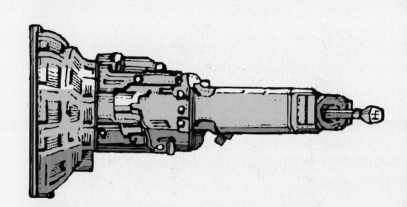

THE TRANSMISSION SYSTEM

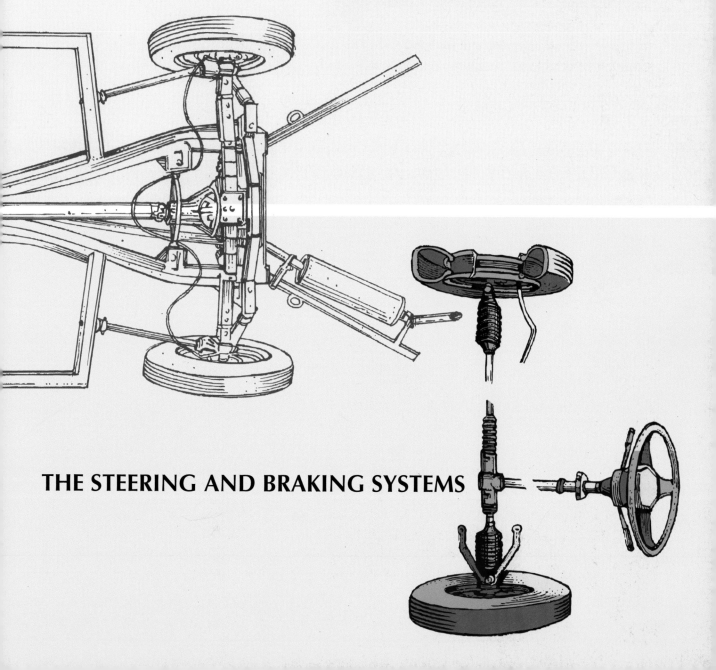

THE STEERING AND BRAKING SYSTEMS

CRANK IT UP

In the early days, car engines had to be cranked by hand to start them. This could be dangerous, however. It required a lot of strength to turn the engine with the crank, and if the vehicle backfired, the crank would turn with sudden force and serious injury could occur. The first "auto-starter" was perfected by Charles Kettering, who had earlier invented a small electric motor to replace the hand crank on cash registers. General Motors heard of his work and commissioned his Dayton Engineering Laboratories Company (Delco) to devise a complete ignition and electrical system for cars, of which the auto-starter became a part. General Motors introduced Kettering's auto-starter in the 1912 Cadillac.

The speed at which the crankshaft spins is measured in revolutions per minute (RPMs). Most drivers run their engines at three to five thousand RPMs.

power flows from the battery to the starter, which cranks the engine. The starter turns the crankshaft, the driving force of the whole engine, and it is kept turning by the pistons, which are like the pedals on a bicycle.

There are many types of internal combustion engines – two-stroke, four-stroke, and rotary are just three examples – but most modern cars still use the four-stroke engine first developed by Nicolaus Otto in 1867 because it's efficient, relatively inexpensive, and easy to refuel.

Pistons are the heart of most car engines, and they move back and forth within a cylinder (this is called reciprocating). Each piston is connected to the crankshaft by a connecting rod.

To complete each cycle, a four-stroke reciprocating engine uses four movements of the piston: 1. the intake stroke; 2. the compression stroke; 3. the combustion/power stroke; 4. the exhaust stroke.

During the intake stroke, the piston moves down the cylinder and creates a partial vacuum. This draws air and fuel through the inlet valve into the cylinder. During this stroke, the exhaust valve stays closed.

When the driver puts her foot on the accelerator, it lets more gasoline and air into the engine. Since most cars have computerized fuel-delivery systems, instead of carburetors, the amount of air let in and fuel released is carefully calculated.

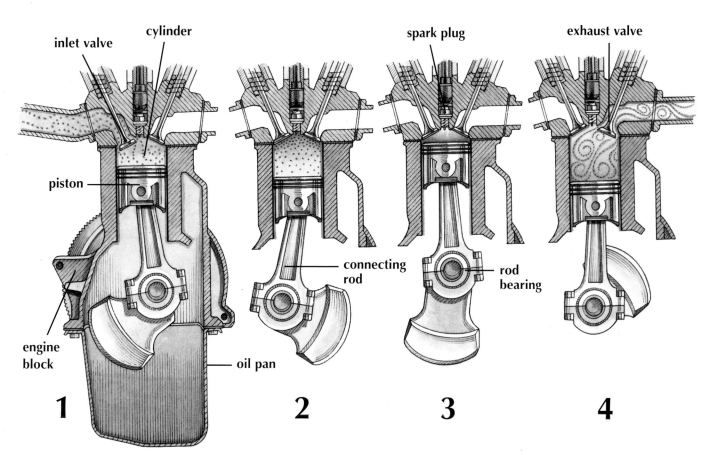

inlet valve **cylinder** **spark plug** **exhaust valve**

piston

connecting rod

rod bearing

engine block

oil pan

1 **2** **3** **4**

The four strokes of the modern internal combustion engine: the intake stroke (fig. 1); the compression stroke (fig. 2); the combustion stroke (fig. 3); and the exhaust stroke (fig. 4).

With the second stroke, the compression stroke, the piston moves up in the cylinder with both valves closed. The air-and-fuel mixture is compressed and the pressure rises.

Just before the end of the compression stroke, the air-and-fuel mixture is ignited by an electric spark from the spark plug. This causes a carefully contained explosion that forces the piston down again, for the third stroke.

THE ELECTRICAL SYSTEM

The car battery stores enough electrical energy from the car's alternator – which is a small generator that produces alternating current – to start the car. It sends voltage to the fuel-injection system, the starter, and the spark plugs. It also powers the windshield wipers, lights, power windows, radio, and so on. Once the car is running, the alternator takes over. It is powered directly by the engine, and it provides current to the whole ignition system. Your car also has fuses that help keep the electrical current working.

IS THE GAS-POWERED CAR RUNNING OUT OF GAS?

In 1900, at the first National Automobile Show in New York City, visitors overwhelmingly chose the electric car as the vehicle of tomorrow, dismissing the smelly and loud gasoline engine as a passing fad. Now it's just the reverse. Gasoline-powered engines have improved so much over the past one hundred years that electric cars have lost their appeal – especially because a gasoline-powered car can go much farther on a tank of fuel than an electric car can go between battery charges. But growing concern about the chemicals that gasoline-powered engines release into the air has led consumers to show more interest in cleaner, more efficient hybrid (gas/electric) cars, as well as cars that run on natural gas and methanol. The once heavily promoted electric car is quietly being abandoned because of its poor safety record, high cost, heavy weight, and short running time. But as we'll see in Chapter 6, many alternative systems and fuel sources are now being developed.

In the fourth stroke, the piston moves up again and forces the burned gases out of the cylinder and into the exhaust system, ridding the chamber of the exhaust. This cycle repeats itself until the ignition is turned off.

There are many different sizes and configurations of car engines. Engine size is usually measured by the amount of air pushed out from all the cylinders as the pistons move from their lowest position to their highest. Engines are also given horsepower ratings. These are a measure of the power they produce and don't necessarily relate to engine size. Generally, most small, economy cars are equipped with 100- to 140-horsepower, four-cylinder engines.

An engine's cylinders can be arranged in different patterns in the engine block. Most often, they are either in a row (referred to as "in-line") or in the shape of a V. The most common arrangements are either 1-4 (which is an in-line engine with four cylinders in a straight row) or V6 (six cylinders in the shape of a V, with three on each side). The V-shape block is popular because it's shorter and can support a heavy crankshaft, which means less vibration and maximum horsepower in a relatively small space.

So now that we've got the engine running smoothly, let's look at how engine power creates "wheel" power.

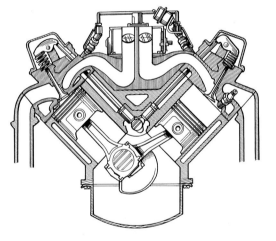

A cross-section of a typical V8 engine. The V6 and the V8 are the most popular V-engines in North America, though Jaguar also makes a V12.

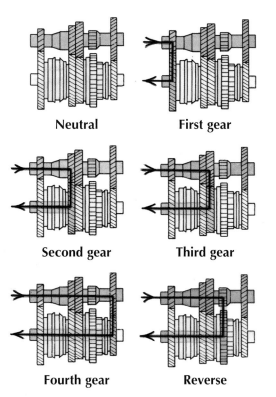

Neutral   **First gear**

Second gear   **Third gear**

Fourth gear   **Reverse**

The arrows show which gears engage at the different speeds.

The Transmission System

As the name suggests, a car's transmission "transmits," or sends, power from the engine to the wheels. Essentially, a car moves forward through a combination of speed and torque, or twisting power. The transmission sets these two characteristics so that the driver gets the smoothest, most efficient ride at the speed she wants. A car climbing a hill, for example, needs more torque to maintain the same speed, while a car coasting along a flat surface at a moderate pace requires less speed and less torque. If a car had no transmission system, it would be difficult for the vehicle to make the best use of all the possible combinations of speed and torque. This would compromise the efficiency of the engine.

So how does the transmission actually work? Well, with each small explosion in the four-stroke engine, a connecting rod turns the crankshaft, sending power through the transmission to a set of gears that adjust the speed and torque to meet the conditions of the road. Whether you have a manual or an automatic transmission, the principle is the same: higher gears allow the engine to run more slowly on long or flat stretches of road, and lower gears help the engine turn faster to produce

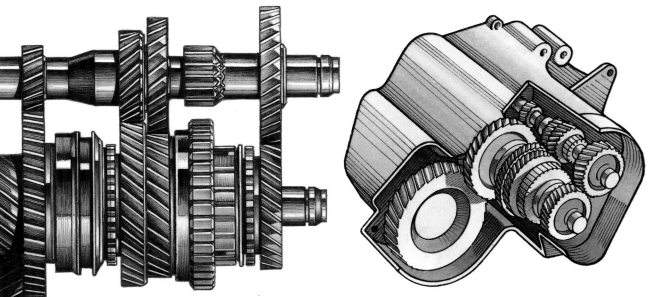

This close-up of the transmission system shows how gears of different sizes correspond to the gear speeds shown above. The teeth are on an angle so they can ease into each other and will make less noise when they engage.

The gears are encased in a housing that protects them and prolongs their life.

WHAT IS THE OCTANE RATING SYSTEM?

Dr. Graham Edgar developed the octane rating system in 1926 to measure the ability of a fuel to burn cleanly. Higher-octane gasoline burns in a way that pushes the piston down smoothly during the power stroke. Lower-octane fuel burns too rapidly, and that can make a knocking or pinging sound in the cylinder, which can harm the engine. You maximize fuel economy and get the cleanest emissions by using the octane rating recommended in your car's owner manual. (Eighty-seven and 90 are the normal ratings for everyday unleaded gasoline.) Unfortunately, misinformed car owners often switch to higher-octane gas in an attempt to rid their car of foul-smelling exhaust fumes or as a "treat" for the engine. Don't be fooled! When you refuel with a gasoline rated higher than your vehicle requires, you are wasting your money and sending unburned fuel into the emissions system, damaging key components and risking more rotten-egg smells.

more power and conserve fuel. In manual transmission, the driver has to shift gears when she wants to increase or decrease her rate of speed. With an automatic transmission, invented in 1937, the gears are shifted automatically. Other popular transmission variants found on today's cars allow for both a manual and an automatic mode, as well as a fifth gear for better fuel efficiency at higher speeds.

Interestingly, 90 percent of cars sold in North America come with automatic transmissions; only 19 percent of cars sold in Europe are automatic. Increased fuel efficiency and tradition give manual transmissions the edge in Europe.

Steering and Braking

The most obvious part of the steering mechanism, the steering wheel, is mainly used to control the car's wheels. But it's just one part of a whole steering system, which is powered by hydraulics, belts, and gears.

Your steering wheel is connected to the end of a steering shaft that runs through a firewall and all the way down to two tie rods that are attached to the front wheels of your car. At the end of the steering shaft is flat gear called a rack and a circular gear called a pinion. When you turn the steering wheel, the pinion also turns and its teeth grip the rack, pushing

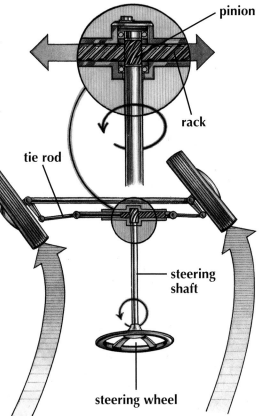

This closeup of the steering column shows how the rack-and-pinion system moves the tie rods from side to side.

it left or right. That, in turn, moves the tie rods, which then move the wheels. This is commonly known as rack-and-pinion steering. There are other forms of steering, of course, but all provide the same result – you can turn your car with ease!

The brake is what you apply to stop the car from moving. Given that the average car weighs more than three thousand pounds (almost 1,400 kilograms), it is amazing how well the brakes work! In recent years, brake design has changed greatly. In the oldest design – known as drum brakes – two semi-circular shoes press outward against the inner surfaces of a steel drum embedded within the tire. That pressure eventually brings the car to a halt. Today, disc brakes are more commonly used on cars – at least on the two front wheels. With these brakes, calipers press against a spinning rotor, or plate, much the way brake pads on a bicycle press against each side of a wheel's rim to slow the bike down. Originally developed for race cars, disc brakes are lighter and offer better braking performance than the drum variety. More expensive cars usually boast disc brakes on all four wheels.

The two types of braking systems. The illustration on the left shows a hand exerting pressure to stop a spinning plate in exactly the same way as the calipers of your disc brakes press against a rotor to slow and eventually stop your tires. On the right, the shoes of your drum brakes press against a steel drum embedded within your tire. Once again, this pressure slows your tires down and eventually brings them to a stop.

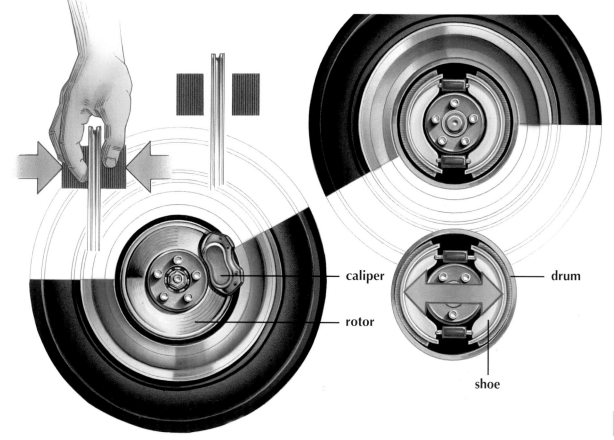

caliper

rotor

drum

shoe

WHAT MAKES A TIRE?

Although rubber is the primary material in tires, a number of other substances are used as well.
These are combined with rubber compounds in the different components that make up the tire.

The tire casing is the body of the tire. Large steel cords that are wound together to form a
cable secure the tire to the wheel and maintain its shape. A belt system is placed on top of the
casing and provides stability to the tread area of the tire, which curbs wear and aids in handling.
A special rubber compound is used in the sidewall to add flexibility and weathering resistance.
The inner liner is also a rubber compound; it's used as an air seal. Weights are attached to the
wheel rims to ensure balance, and rubber treads provide traction. The treads also give water
somewhere to go – other than between the surface of the tire and the road. This is why it is so
very important to check tread wear. Many people recommend the tried-and-true method of
inserting a penny into the tread with the head pointed down. If you can see the top of Lincoln's
or the Queen's head, you know it's time to get new tires! The trick works because the distance between
the rim and Lincoln's or the Queen's head is 1/16 of an inch – the minumum required thread depth.

The Chassis and the Suspension System

Chassis (pronounced TCHA-see or SHA-see) is the French
word for "frame." At one time, it simply referred to the frame
of the car, which was what the body, engine, driveline components, and suspension system were attached to. In effect, the
chassis provided the strength of the car. Now few vehicles other
than trucks have separate frames, and the chassis structure –
which is a semi-flexible group of mounts, struts, joints, and
stabilizing bars that provide structural support– is incorporated
into the body in what is known as a shell (or unit-body)
construction. However, the word is still what most people use
when they're referring to a car's frame. Even if it's no longer
a separate entity, it still holds everything together!

Attached to the lower frame of the car is the suspension
system, which cushions your ride and keeps the car from
swaying and jerking too much – and spilling your coffee. The
suspension system uses bars, dampers, and springs to help the
car adjust to variations in the road. Apart from giving a more
comfortable ride, this also protects the car from bumps and
dings and makes the steering easier to control.

Power steering uses hydraulic
pressure created by the engine
to help you maneuver your
car. Your vehicle will be much
harder to steer if it is low on
power-steering fluid or if the
steering gears and bushings
are too worn. In both cases,
the steering wheel will be
hard to turn when you start
out on cold mornings, but it
will return to normal once
you're under way. Don't be
fooled into thinking the problem has gone away, however.
It needs your immediate
attention because it will get
worse and cost more to fix
the longer you wait to act.

Anti-lock brakes, or ABS, were once promoted as a feature safety-conscious drivers couldn't do without. But just how safe are they? Researchers now report that stopping distance isn't necessarily shortened with ABS, and the brakes fail so frequently that the U.S. government's Department of Transportation says they represent the second-largest category of safety complaints.

The Cooling System

A running engine generates enough heat to destroy itself, but the cooling system won't let that happen. Using a mixture of coolant and air, it ensures that combustion doesn't overheat the engine, causing the metal to warp or crack. The coolant, called antifreeze, is water mixed with a bit of ethylene glycol, a chemical that keeps the water from freezing at low temperatures. It's used year-round, mostly because it has rust-inhibiting qualities that can be beneficial even in the summer. It's also more convenient to use antifreeze in both winter and summer – you don't need to switch between it and plain water as the seasons change (though a radiator flush should be done once every two years).

The fan pumps coolant through the engine, the radiator, and the heater to protect those parts from getting damaged by overheating. As it goes through the engine, the coolant absorbs the heat and carries it to the radiator. There, the fan draws air

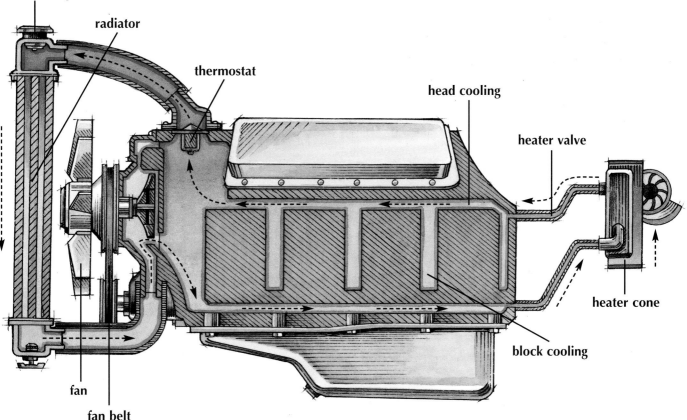

radiator cap

radiator

thermostat

head cooling

heater valve

heater cone

block cooling

fan

fan belt

through the coolant, "radiating" the heat away. It's sort of like blowing on a bowl of hot soup to cool it down.

Sometimes, you can hear a whirring noise when the engine is shut off. That means that the fan is still cooling down the engine. If the fan belt breaks, you will lose engine power, steering and braking will be more difficult, and electrical power will be seriously reduced.

Oil is another part of the cooling system. It keeps the engine's internal parts running with a minimum of friction. Too much friction can cause the engine to overheat, and that will result in warping of the engine parts, cracks in the engine block, or leaks in the engine head gasket. Synthetic oil is a slipperier kind of oil that is said to make your engine run better – but it is quite expensive and may void the auto manufacturer's warranty.

So now that we understand the basics of how cars operate, let's take a look at how they are designed. After all, if it doesn't look good, no one will care how well it runs!

CHAPTER 3

CAR DESIGN: FROM FUNCTION TO STYLE

Did you ever make a car out of play dough or doodle your very own dream machine? Did you know that automobile manufacturers employ full-time designers to "play around" with mundane vehicle designs and devise hot new concept cars? Maybe that's the job for you. These designers often have degrees in engineering or industrial design or have graduated from transportation design schools, and they almost always were crazy about cars as kids!

Car Designers: The Rock Stars of the Auto Industry?

Since all car manufacturers have access to basically the same technology and engineering expertise, it is the designers who make the difference. They provide the vision for new models that will capture the hearts of the car-buying public. Ever since General Motors first used annual styling improvements to lure Ford buyers away from the staid Model T, automakers have known that how a car looks is just as important a factor as how it runs when buyers are trying to decide between one model and another. In fact, manufacturers compete to attract "star" designers much as sports teams will recruit hot new talent or "franchise" players.

The fixation on design has intensified in the past few decades. When industry regulations changed in the 1970s and 1980s, vehicles had to have stronger bodies and offer improved

THE ISETTA: WHERE STYLE AND FUNCTION COLLIDE

Das rollende Ei (German for "the rolling egg"), as the Isetta was affectionately called, was originally manufactured by a refrigerator company called ISO in Italy in 1953. But the car did not sell well, so ISO sold both the design and the manufacturing rights to BMW in 1955. With a little restyling, BMW produced a car with more power and convenience, and the Isetta was finally a success.

The Isetta was one of the true "bubble cars," which means that it had a bubble-shaped body that was made from steel and bolted to a separate tubular chassis. These cars burst onto the European auto scene in the 1950s, answering the demand for low-cost, weatherproof personal transportation. Names like Messerschmitt, Heinkel, Goggomobil, and Isetta began to appear on these tiny, usually three-wheeled cars. They were a step up from a motorcycle and sidecar, which is what many people were using for family transportation at the time.

But the Isetta was certainly not your run-of-the-mill two-passenger car. Perhaps the original manufacturer, Renzo Rivolta, was influenced by his refrigerators when he designed it, because the entire front of the car, including the windshield, swung out like an appliance door, bringing the universal-jointed steering column with it.

Unfortunately, the Isetta was definitely not freeway friendly, and large potholes would swallow the tiny ten-inch (25 centimeter) wheels. Visibility was excellent, however; people said it was like driving in a fishbowl! Parking was also a snap, and fuel economy was tremendous. Perhaps that's why the short-lived popularity of this car helped BMW pull back from the brink of bankruptcy. Today, the "mini car" is enjoying a renaissance. The BMW Mini Cooper is particularly popular in huge metropolises like New York City, where owners are enthusiastic about its ability to dart in and out of tight traffic and find parking spaces that no SUV could ever fit into!

fuel economy. Manufacturers responded by developing cars of a fairly uniform design. The gas-guzzling "muscle cars" of the 1960s could no longer tear down the highways. Designers aimed for economy and space in most models, and this resulted in cars that came to be called Euro boxes (for the standard three-part plan of engine, cabin, trunk, which allowed for maximum space in the most economical design). These efficient but uninspiring boxes on wheels dominated the car market through the 1980s.

Each year, design students from Canada, China, France, Japan, England, Italy, Korea, India, Sweden, and the United States take part in the World Automotive Design Competition. Their challenge is to create an economical vehicle that reflects the country where they live or study. Leading automotive designers from around the world act as judges, and winners are announced at the Canadian International Auto Show each February.

In the 1990s, car designers continued to strive to be environmentally friendly, but they also wanted to generate excitement about cars as an enhancement to the driver's lifestyle. Sleek and streamlined "jellybean" styling was made possible with the development of new body materials, such as fiberglass, polyurethane, and carbon fiber. Using computers, designers shaped these new materials into lightweight, durable, and angled body panels that have opened up a new era of possibilities. These ultra-light materials also contribute to better gas mileage, a feature that all but the most affluent and environmentally unfriendly driver strives for.

Nevertheless, in today's crowded market, the desire to stand out is what drives auto manufacturers. For that reason, design is a critical component in the marketing and selling of automobiles. Because the quality gap between the various makes has largely closed, brand imagery and design are almost all that's left when it comes to differentiating between vehicles. Marketers call it selling the sizzle, not the steak.

Developing New Designs

Creating a new car model takes many years and a lot of money. Automobile manufacturers invest several billion dollars in research and development to ensure that they come up with a kind of car that consumers will want to buy. Before the design work even begins, researchers monitor economics, social changes, age groups, needs, and even fashion trends. Cost targets must also be set before the initial concept for a new car can be determined. Endless changes occur during the development stages – some prompted by logic, others by intuition or serendipity. This carries through the entire design process and production planning.

Computer-aided design (CAD) systems help engineers and designers create a new style, and this is then tested exhaustively before it ever reaches the market. These sophisticated software programs allow designers to build computerized models of almost anything (car bodies, engines, drivetrains, transmission and exhaust systems, gas-flow patterns, etc.) and then manipulate them, simulate them, and refine them. And since someone

START YOUR ENGINES!

The impact of CAD on the automobile industry is not limited to exterior design. Companies are using the software to optimize the engine and develop alternative fuel sources (such as hybrid, electric, fuel cell, and solar) – just a few of the ways they are trying to improve their cars' performance.

In 1995, Chevrolet came out with an engine called the SB2. Using CAD, designers were able to increase the size of the engine and optimize the location of its intake and exhaust valves, as well as maximizing the airflow in the manifolds to get more power without adding weight. They were even able to do this within the approved guidelines of NASCAR, displacing an engine type that had not been changed since 1955. The SB2 powered the legendary Chevrolet Monte Carlo, which has been driven by many winners of the NASCAR Winston Cup since 1995.

is always devising better technology for cars – from anti-lock brakes to airbags – it's crucial to have cutting-edge software like CAD that can reduce the time car companies need to incorporate advancements into new lines.

Yet as useful as many software programs are, there are some things that cannot be left to virtual reality alone. That is why new car models are put through all sorts of accident scenarios and severe-weather testing in desert and Arctic climes. Intense market research involving focus groups and other user testing allows for invaluable consumer input. In addition, auto manufacturers routinely dissect the products of their competitors, looking for secrets they can adapt or pitfalls they can avoid in their quest to come up with the next big thing. And perhaps the biggest hurdle for every new car concept is the scrutiny of its own company – executive veto power has been known to kill many promising car models. With fortunes riding on the success or failure of every new entry into the marketplace, it is no wonder that any designer who has a solid record of producing top-selling car models is treated like an all-star athlete!

Passing the Test – and the Competition!

Every designer dreams of creating a car model that will be a future "classic." Yet even the best-designed cars can flop for

Automobile manufacturers use cutting-edge technology for more than just designing new cars. General Motors played a key role in the creation of the Dodrill-GMR Heart Machine, a mechanical heart that resembles a miniature automobile engine. Credited with saving more than 750,000 lives, the machine was developed by Dr. Forrest Dewey Dodrill and General Motors Research in 1952.

Many people painted their Bricklins – with disastrous results if the body wasn't properly prepared first. The car's acrylic composition, gull-wing doors, and aerodynamic styling may all have been too far ahead of their time.

reasons that aren't always easy to explain. Take, for example, the Bricklin and the DeLorean, both of which were uniquely styled sportscars introduced with great fanfare.

The Bricklin SV-1 was built in New Brunswick, Canada, by Malcolm Bricklin, an American entrepreneur, between 1974 and 1976. Distinguished by its unpainted acrylic body and gull-wing doors, the Bricklin was manufactured primarily from Detroit parts for exclusive sale in the United States. The futuristic vehicle was initially very well liked by owners and the automotive press, but it suffered from a series of production problems and was never manufactured in large enough numbers to be profitable. The plant closed in 1976, when the New Brunswick government withdrew its funding support and the company went bankrupt.

You could say that the technology of the time simply did not support the imaginativeness of the car's design. The novelty of the unpainted body quickly became an annoyance, for example, because the exterior panels (made of fiberglass and acrylic, components that would expand at different rates) would swell if exposed to hot sun for long periods, causing leaks and other problems. And although the gull wings were "space age," they took ten seconds to open and the dramatic effect soon wore thin. Water leaks, hydraulic-system fires, and a poorly ventilated passenger compartment joined the long list of other defects that eroded the car's many charms. In fact, with so many technical glitches, the Bricklin, which was originally expected to supplant the Corvette, is now deemed a Canadian "lemon" of historic proportions!

Ironically, the car exceeded the safety requirements of the time (there was no ashtray or cigarette lighter either!); the designation SV-1 stood for Safety Vehicle 1. It had a built-in roll cage, side guard rails, and shock-absorbing bumpers that receded into the car. It was not only safe in an accident but had the power and handling to avoid one.

Introduced five years after the Bricklin plant was closed down, the DeLorean was manufactured in Northern Ireland by the DeLorean Motor Company (DMC). The car was origi-nally intended for the U.S. market, and only a few were sold elsewhere in the world. (A series was also produced for the

John DeLorean is still regarded as one of America's most innovative automotive designers, despite the colossal failure of the car that bore his name.

FIFTY YEARS OF CAR DESIGNS

In the past fifty years, car designers have had far more misses than hits. Here are our top picks for the best- and worst-designed cars from those five decades. See if you agree.

THE GOOD

1963 Corvette Stingray – Dropped after only one year in production, this Corvette has a unique split rear windshield.

1964 Ford Mustang convertible – This inexpensive little sportscar debuted at the New York World's Fair and was an instant hit with car fanatics, who loved its affordability and its high style.

1959 Cadillac convertible – A dinosaur with tail fins, Harley Earle's stylish giant deftly combines heft with horsepower and chrome with cachet.

THE BAD

Trabant – This East German car was originally meant to be a closed motorbike. Its plastic-and-fiberglass body housed an engine that could reach a top speed of only fifty-five miles (90 kilometers) an hour. Unreliable and unwanted, the Trabi is a relic of Germany's Communist past.

VW Beetle – The Beetle may have got your mom and dad through college during the 1970s, but it was never designed for winter driving. Heaters were something Beetle owners could only dream of, and the front-mounted fuel tank made the car a firetrap. But it was cheap.

1971–77 GM Vega – This failure-prone, biodegradable car had a shoe-horned engine that you lifted out to change the spark plugs. The one-time Chevrolet executive John DeLorean said the car's engine was "a relatively large, noisy, top-heavy combination of aluminum and iron which cost far too much to build [and] looked like it had been taken off a 1920 farm tractor."

1984–88 GM Fiero – This fire-prone, unreliable sportscar wannabe looked better than it performed.

THE UGLY

2000–2005 Aztek – An SUV built on a minivan platform, the Aztek has a hideous front end and a huge, angular rear. It's an ungainly vehicle that appalls more than appeals.

1948–64 Messerschmidt – This German-built three-wheeler had tandem seating (passenger behind driver), twist-grip throttles, a hand-operated clutch, and no Reverse gear.

1975–80 Pacer – A wide, egg-shaped car, the Pacer earned itself several dubious nicknames, including "the rolling greenhouse" and "the pregnant guppy."

DaimlerChrysler Smart – A Mercedes go-cart, the Smart is a trunkless two-seater powered by a three-cylinder engine. It flipped over twice at its own "moose-avoidance" press conference. When not on its back, this inexpensive micro-car has a top speed of eighty-four miles (135 kilometers) an hour.

Canadian market.) There were about 9,200 of the unique cars manufactured during the two years the company was in production, and many of them are still in use by car enthusiasts today. The DeLorean featured gull-wing doors and a stainless steel exterior that required no paint. It had safety features similar to those of the Bricklin, such as side-impact protection and re-formable bumpers. The unique design gave the car a futuristic look that is probably best identified with the popular *Back to the Future* movies starring Michael J. Fox.

Although there are numerous theories regarding the closure of the DeLorean plant in Ireland, it was likely the result of several factors, including a weak market, unfavorable exchange rates, and unforeseen cost overruns. The car also had serious defects that contributed to its demise, such as steering failures and binding, doors jamming and bending, and windshield stress cracks. Today the car's dynamic appearance and features keep it at the top of the heap with classic car collectors.

The Art of Design

Today's designers are far less likely to come up with lemons of the magnitude of the Bricklin or the DeLorean. Technology advancements and intense market research help guard against massive flubs. But respect for traditional design approaches

HARLEY EARLE'S "KILLER" FINS

Harley Earle was a gifted GM designer who started the fad for rear tail fins. These were later decried as "killers" in Ralph Nader's 1965 book *Unsafe at Any Speed* because the protruding fins became lethal weapons in accidents. Earle believed that style was just as important as function, however. When other automakers brought out safer, smaller, and more economical cars, Earle stuck by his fins, and GM's market share began a long decline. Today, Earle is lionized by the company as a design genius.

Designers are sometimes asked to "reincarnate" cars like the GT40, a legendary racer built to challenge Ferrari at the Le Mans 24-Hour Race in the mid-1960s. Named for its forty-inch (100 centimeter) height, the original GT40 began life as a paper-napkin drawing. It was then rendered through clay models executed by the chief designer. Today, the "new" GT40 is part of Ford's "Living Legends" lineup of production and concept cars; other "legends" are the Thunderbird, the Mustang, and the Forty-Nine concept car.

endures, and not everyone is mad about CAD. European car designers continue to favor the clay-model approach to design because they believe computer-aided designs result in a "sea of anonymous metal."

It was actually an American, Harley Earle, who first used life-sized clay models of new designs. He worked for General Motors from the late 1920s to the 1950s and has been described as the first professional car designer. Some even believe that because General Motors recognized the value of style over function, Ford eventually lost its monopoly over the North American car market. A sea of black cars might have been efficient from a production perspective (don't forget that black paint takes less time to dry), but with the growing popularity of the automobile as a primary mode of transportation, it didn't take very long for manufacturers to understand the need for a competitive edge.

Today, American companies still use clay models to demonstrate important new designs to key in-house decision-makers, but unlike their European counterparts, they tend to introduce these models at the end of the design process, not the beginning. However, automobile designers around the world recognize the advantages of using three-dimensional digital computer modeling. It is much easier to collaborate on detail design for specific car parts when digital images can be relayed quickly and information pooled for everyone on the design team to access. This is probably why the trend for retro design has taken off. As we have seen, many cars of the 1960s and 1970s were simply ahead of their time. Thanks to the technology revolution that has taken place since then, carmakers now have the ability to turn former lemons into lemonade!

Concept Cars and Crossovers

Carmakers use concepts to spark interest in their mainline offerings and to capture news "hits" on slow days. Concept vehicles are often called dream cars because they are design exercises that may not ever make it to the mainstream market. Just as fashion designers unveil each year's new lines with over-the-top fashion shows, car companies unveil these

pre-production prototypes at auto shows around the world, where they are used to draw attention from industry watchers and the public. If they meet with favorable response, these concept cars may proceed to market, but by the time they hit the car lots, they are often in a much-altered state. Still, concept cars are important, for they give us hints about where the automotive industry is headed. Often, these heavily hyped cars are a fundamental part of the development plans of the leading lights of the car industry.

Crossover cars fulfill the consumer's desire to have a single vehicle play the role of many. In the 1970s, the fuel crisis drove designers to develop cars that were much smaller – and therefore more fuel-efficient – than before. In much the same way, today's car gurus are challenged to come up with designs that

From blueprint to blacktop: Concept cars are the forerunners of the models that will be on the road in a few years.

WHAT'S IN A NAME?

Ever wonder how the international automobile giants got their names? Here's the story behind some of the biggest.

DAIMLER (Germany): Gottlieb Daimler (1834–1900) designed the first workable four-stroke internal combustion engine, and the Daimler Motoren Gesellschaft was founded in 1890 to produce cars. The British Daimler Company was formed later; it purchased the U.K. rights from the German company and built cars using Daimler engines.

FORD (America): Henry Ford (1863–1947) first set up the Henry Ford Company in 1901. It became the Ford Motor Company in 1903, and it continues to be the most recognizable of the industry pioneers.

HONDA (Japan): Soichiro Honda (1906–1991) was a mechanic who founded Honda in 1948. The company originally produced motorcycles; Honda cars were introduced in 1964.

MERCEDES: Emil Jellinek was the Austro-Hungarian consul in France, and he was given the right to sell Daimler's cars in Austria, Hungary, France, and the United States. Mercedes, the name Jellinek chose for Daimler's cars in those markets, was in fact the name of his daughter. Daimler liked the name Mercedes so much that in 1902 the company registered it as its car trademark.

MORRIS (U.K.): William Richard Morris (1877–1963) started off as a bicycle repairer near Oxford. He went into the business of building motorcycles in 1901, and then built the first Morris Oxford in 1913.

TOYOTA (Japan): Sakichi Toyoda (1894–1952) invented the automatic loom in 1925, and a year later he formed the Toyoda Automatic Loom Works Ltd. The company eventually diversified into cars, and the first Toyoda was produced by Kiichiro Toyoda, Sakichi's son, in 1935. The name of the company was changed to the Toyota Motor Company in 1937.

reflect drivers' sometimes conflicting interests. For example, many people want more space in their vehicles, but they don't want added length. "Crossover design" is a term that can be used to describe vehicles that are part truck and part car, part SUV and part sportscar – multi-functional designs that speak to the complex needs of modern drivers.

Looking Ahead

Where do designers see the automotive industry ten years from now? Most would welcome a greater focus on alternative fuels. It also seems likely that the car industry will continue to endorse "retro" stylings by designers who reclaim classic models and inject new life into them with modern technology.

Now that you understand how cars are designed, let's look at what you need to know about them after they have been successfully introduced to the consumer. Here's where your dreams of driving your own car start to become a reality!

CHAPTER 4

WHAT MAKES A GOOD CAR?

Remember Harry Potter's Uncle Vernon? Intensely materialistic, he tended to judge other men by how big and expensive their cars were. Unfortunately, the world is full of Uncle Vernons – and that's why the upscale car market is alive and well. For those who can afford it, it is possible to buy a car in the range of $300,000 to $900,000! But most of us are not looking for luxury features or futuristic gadgets. No, safety and reliability are what most people want in a good car.

How to Avoid Picking a Lemon

Like friends, some cars are more reliable than others. Industry insiders say that one-tenth of the cars produced each year will turn out to be lemons. Fortunately, there is a lot of trustworthy information available to help you and your family avoid choosing one. Annual industry lists rank everything from engine technology and the top safety features to the cheapest and most expensive cars to run. Each year, North American consumer experts also publish listings of the most and least reliable cars. And newspapers and magazines regularly summarize the best and worst cars reviewed by their auto critics. *Consumer Reports* magazine (published by Consumers Union, an American consumer-advocacy group) even selects the most uncomfortable cars and trucks for tall and short drivers!

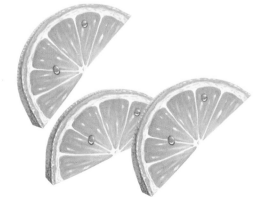

WHAT IS A LEMON?

A "lemon" is a vehicle that is unsafe, unreliable, beyond repair, or unfit to drive. American state lemon laws define a lemon as a vehicle that has a problem that cannot be repaired after three or four tries. (Canada doesn't have lemon legislation.)

Some industry analysts estimate that one out of every ten Detroit Big Three vehicles is a lemon, a figure echoed by Chrysler's former president, Robert Lutz, who told *The Chrysler Times* in 1995, "Out of one hundred vehicles, we're apt to build ten that are as good as any that Toyota has ever built, eighty that are okay and ten that cause repeated problems for our customers."

Consumer Reports, a magazine that tests products and alerts consumers to good and bad buys, polled almost half a million subscribers in 2002 and found that Japanese brands led the industry for quality. Luxury automakers such as Cadillac and Mercedes-Benz got the worst ratings, from a quality standpoint. In a summary of the best- and poorest-quality vehicles, the magazine found that the Acura RL, the Honda Civic and CR-V, the Lexus ES300, the Mazda Miata, and the Toyota Camry had the fewest factory-related defects. The vehicles with the most defects were the Chevrolet Corvette and Astro/Safari, the Ford Focus, the Mercedes-Benz M-Class, and Volkswagen's Golf/Jetta and New Beetle.

Interestingly, the British consumer magazine *Which?* reported in its September 2001 issue that not even half of British car owners would recommend a British-made Rover or Vauxhall to a friend. The most highly rated cars in that study were the Japanese-made Subaru, Isuzu, and Lexus – recommended by more than 85 percent of drivers.

Where can all this information be found? A visit to your local public library is an excellent place to start. Most libraries will carry the annual Lemon-Aid consumer car guides and monthly magazines like *Consumer Reports*. You can find links to these publications and many other excellent national and international resources on the Internet. Check the "Where to Look" section at the back of this book for advice on how to find these and other good sources of consumer information.

You can check a vehicle's age by consulting the date-of-manufacture plate, which is found on the driver's-side door pillar. If, for example, the date of manufacture is 7/04, your vehicle was one of the last 2004 models made before the September changeover to the 2005 models. That's a good thing, since your vehicle will have benefited from almost a year of production improvements.

However, you must be cautious with any information you get off the Internet, carefully verifying its source, because not all of it is truthful or has been generated by independent experts. Many so-called ranking lists are actually nothing more than fake media releases posted by car companies to promote their own products! (In the "Where to Look" section, you'll find a checklist to follow when using the Internet for research.) You should also be a little wary of newspaper and magazine articles. They can be helpful, but because car columnists are given access to free test vehicles, some have trouble remaining objective and will simply summarize automakers' marketing and promotional materials. This is why you don't read a lot about things like crashworthiness, parts pricing and availability, warranty complaints, and depreciation when automotive journalists rate new vehicles.

Most critics would agree, however, that buying a new vehicle during its first year on the market is not a good idea. Why wait? Well, every model is gradually improved each year it's in production, so the car's quality is actually at its highest level toward the end of its model lifecycle. Newly designed cars get quality scores that are on the average 2 percent lower than those of models that have been around for a while.

Believe it or not, it can even make a difference what time of year you buy your car. Because they were the first off the assembly line for that model year, vehicles made between September and February are called first series cars. They are apt to have more problems than so-called second series cars because glitches in the assembly process have not yet been ironed out. Second series vehicles – those made between March and August – tend to be better built than the earlier models. Although both first and second series cars will sell for the same price, the later ones will be a far better buy. If you're going to buy new, do it after February.

And that's not all! Many people believe that a car's quality can be affected even by which day of the week it comes off the assembly line. In fact, the famous novelist Arthur Hailey, in his bestseller *Wheels*, warned buyers not to purchase an American-built car made on a Monday or a Friday. According

UNCOVERING YOUR CAR'S SECRETS

Every vehicle manufactured anywhere in the world has a story to tell. It's possible to piece that story together through factory data and reliability and safety information. Records even show when and where a car was last serviced, and by which owner. Here are fifteen "hidden" facts you can uncover about your car:

1. Black box recorder – This electronic tattle-tale device can usually be found under the driver's seat or inside the glove compartment. It records many of your driving habits, and it can tell crash investigators how fast you were going and whether the brakes were applied just before a collision.

2. Birthdate plate – This date-of-manufacture plate is found on the driver's-side door pillar.

3. Birthplace sticker – This sticker, also on the driver's door, shows where the vehicle was assembled.

4. Premature corrosion damage – Areas particularly vulnerable to early corrosion damage are door bottoms (often called rocker panels), rear wheel wells, and under-chassis mounts for spare tires on SUVs and other vehicles.

5. Poor-quality, wrong-sized, or underinflated tires – Tire ratings are found on the tire sidewall and are a good indicator of how well the tire will perform. Size and inflation specifications are noted by the auto manufacturer on the driver's door pillar and by the tiremaker on the sidewall. Always follow the automaker's guidelines. Wrong-sized tires or under- or overinflation will dangerously compromise a vehicle's handling.

6. Owner complaints to the government – If you're trying to get an automaker to repair an ongoing problem free of charge, it will help your case if you can produce a record of similar complaints made to the U.S. National Highway Traffic Safety Association (NHTSA).

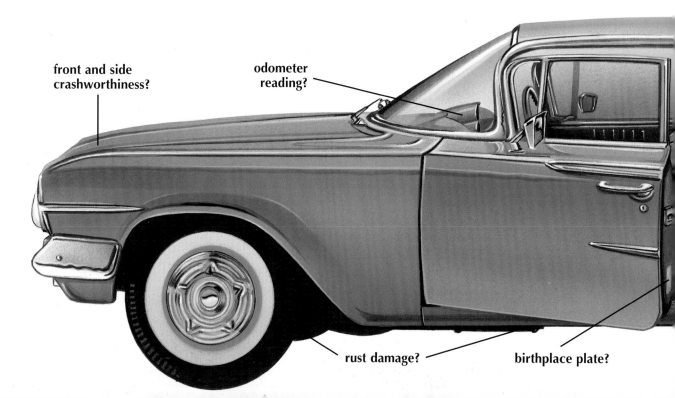

front and side crashworthiness?

odometer reading?

rust damage?

birthplace plate?

7. Confidential service bulletins – The NHTSA and Alldata.com together keep a summary of all the bulletins car manufacturers issue on each model. Use these bulletins to confirm that defects are factory-related and should be fixed for free. Bulletins are also good for showing independent garages where to look to repair a problem.

8. Secret "goodwill" warranties – Information on these free repair programs can usually be found in NHTSA and Alldata.com bulletin summaries under headings like "Special Policies," "Customer Satisfaction Programs," or "Goodwill." These apply only to factory-related defects.

9. Safety probes and recalls – Again, this information from the NHTSA tips you off to free safety-related repairs.

10. Crashworthiness rating – Not all vehicles provide the same occupant crash protection. Check out crashtest.com for a comparative listing of crashworthiness from testing agencies around the world.

11. Head restraint effectiveness – The Insurance Institute for Highway Safety compiles this important data. You can find the institute's website listed at the back of the book.

12. Vehicle's rollover tendency – This NHTSA-supplied data is especially vital to owners of SUVs, trucks, and vans, where rollovers are most common.

13. Previous owners and odometer readings – Any new-car dealer also selling previously owned vehicles of the same brand can pull this information out of his or her computer.

14. Past work performed and outstanding warranties – Again, a same-brand dealer can easily access this information from computer files kept by the manufacturer.

15. Free emissions and warranty work to be done – Any same-brand dealer has access to this information online.

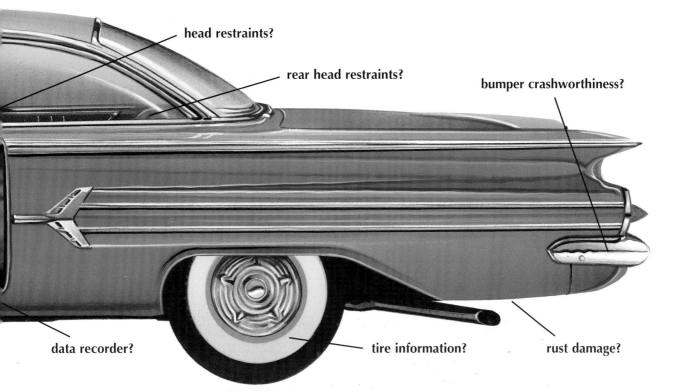

head restraints?

rear head restraints?

bumper crashworthiness?

data recorder?

tire information?

rust damage?

to Hailey, on Mondays many workers are in a bad mood about having to come back to work, and on Fridays everyone just wants to get the heck out of the factory. The end result is a poor job on those two days of the week. Unfortunately, it's impossible for the average buyer to find out what day a car was built. And auto workers themselves say that Monday cars may be no worse than those made just before lunch or quitting time.

What Makes a Good Car?

When consumer critics rate cars, they look for five important things: safety, crashworthiness, durability, good fuel economy, and reasonable maintenance costs. These are key factors in determining a car's quality. Let's look at each one in turn.

When critics look at a car's *safety performance*, they especially want to know how it will respond in emergency situations, such as when a driver needs to suddenly change course or brake without the vehicle going out of control or rolling over. Other features that have been proven to add to a car's safety include seatbelt pretensioners that lock efficiently in a collision; depowered airbags, which deploy in stages or with less force than those made prior to 1997; adjustable brake and accelerator pedals; integrated child safety seats; effective head restraints; traction control; and unhampered front and rear visibility. Side airbags won't be considered a viable safety feature until real-world crash findings prove their worth and confirm that they're not a danger to children, women, seniors, or small-statured adults, as a number of safety researchers have suggested.

A car's *crashworthiness* is its ability to shield occupants from injury-producing forces in a collision. Occupants must be well protected from front, off-set, side, and rear collisions, as well as rollovers. To do this, automakers build a protective "cage" around the occupants with reinforced door beams, roofs, and side pillars.

THE TOP TEN SAFETY DEFECTS
REPORTED BY CAR OWNERS

No matter the make or model, cars that fail tend to fail in the same way. Here's a list of the most common safety defects reported by car owners, according to the U.S. Department of Transportation's National Highway Traffic Safety Administration. How many of these problems can you spot on the car pictured below?

1. Airbags not deploying when they should or deploying when they shouldn't!
2. Total failure of the anti-lock braking system (ABS); wheel lockup.
3. Tire tread separation.
4. Electrical or fuel-system fires.
5. Sudden acceleration.
6. Sudden stalling.
7. Sudden electrical failure.
8. Transmission fails to engage or suddenly disengages.
9. Transmission jumps from Park to Reverse or Neutral; vehicle rolls away when parked.
10. Steering or suspension failure.

WHAT DO ALL THOSE NUMBERS MEAN?

Have you ever had a look at the side of one of your car's tires? Well, all the numbers you can find there serve an important purpose, telling you everything from how much air pressure the tire can bear to the maximum speed it can go. Let's take a closer look at what those numbers mean.

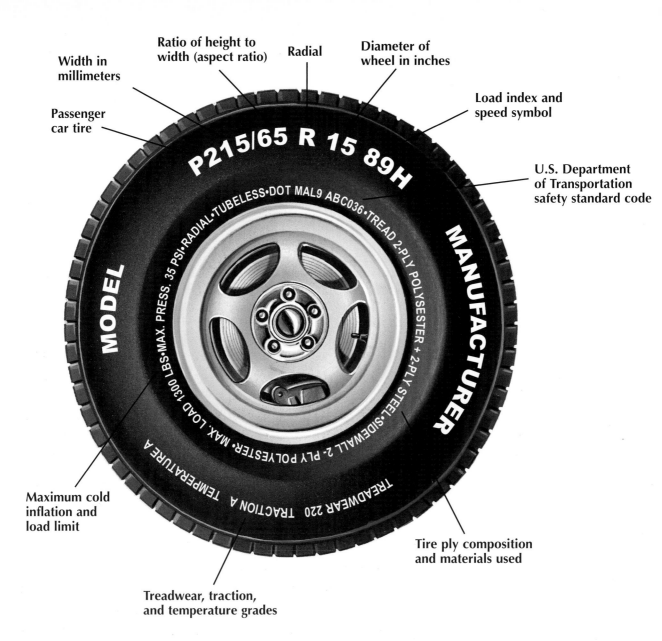

Width in millimeters

Ratio of height to width (aspect ratio)

Radial

Diameter of wheel in inches

Load index and speed symbol

Passenger car tire

U.S. Department of Transportation safety standard code

Maximum cold inflation and load limit

Tire ply composition and materials used

Treadwear, traction, and temperature grades

FUEL ECONOMY CONVERSION CHART

m.p.g.	L/100 km	m.p.g.	L/100 km	m.p.g.	L/100 km	m.p.g.	L/100 km
12	23.0	21	13.5	31	9.0	43	6.7
13	21.0	22	13.0	33	8.5	44	6.4
14	20.0	23	12.5	35	8.0	46	6.2
15	19.0	24	12.0	36	7.8	47	6.0
16	18.0	25	11.5	37	7.6	48	5.8
17	17.0	26	11.0	38	7.4	50	5.6
18	16.0	27	10.5	39	7.2	52	5.4
19	15.0	28	10.0	40	7.0	54	5.2
20	14.0	30	9.5	42	6.8	56	5.0

Almost all cars have these safety features, which are required by federal law; because of styling differences, however, they don't all offer the same crash protection.

Critics also want to know how *durable* a car will be. A top-rated model should easily last ten to fifteen years, be made with a high level of quality, and be reliable. As you read through the quality and reliability ratings found in many auto guides, you'll quickly see that most Japanese automakers and South Korea's Hyundai consistently place far ahead of Chrysler, Ford, GM, and the European manufacturers in maintaining a high level of quality control in their vehicles. What once was a small-car phenomenon has now spread to mid-size and luxury cars, minivans, trucks, and sport utility vehicles, according to both *Consumer Reports* and J. D. Power and Associates, an organization that ranks car models based on customer satisfaction.

Good *fuel economy* and affordable *annual maintenance costs* are also important factors to consider. An economy car should average thirty-five to forty miles to the gallon (8 to 7 liters per 100 kilometers) on the highway. Economical family sedans will give you around twenty-five miles to the gallon (11.5 liters per 100 kilometers), and fuel-efficient full-sized vehicles should get

THE WORLD'S WORST CAR

If you were deliberately to build an unsafe and unreliable car, you would put the gas tank in the front to get a good fire going, forgo head restraints and seatbelts, and make easily collapsible front seatbacks that would launch passengers through a small porthole-like rear windshield in a crash. Hey, that's the original Volkswagen Beetle! Want to make the car failure-prone as well? Give it gull-wing doors and a European powertrain – just like the 1977 DeLorean. Now if you just want to make an ugly car, borrow some design features from American Motors' 1975 Pacer or GM's 2001 Aztek SUV.

around twenty miles to the gallon (14 liters per 100 kilometers). Maintenance shouldn't cost more than eight hundred dollars a year, and parts should be easy to find and reasonably priced.

Cars are also rated on their resale value. After four years, a car's value should be around 50 percent of its original selling price. After ten years, your car should still be worth about a third of its initial value.

Other factors that determine a car's quality include the type of standard equipment offered; the comfort of the driving position; the effectiveness of displays and controls (including climate control); ease of entry and exit; and the amount of interior and cargo space. Although driving pleasure varies from person to person, a cramped interior, controls that are hard to see or reach, poor climate-control systems, and excessive engine, road, and wind noise can turn a pleasurable experience into a distressing one.

What Makes a Bad Car?

A bad car is one that is overpriced, unreliable, and gulps gas. What's worse, it is unsafe to drive, gives little crash protection, rolls over easily, doesn't respond to your driving needs, handles poorly, provides an uncomfortable ride, constantly breaks down, and can't be easily or inexpensively serviced.

That much should be obvious. But even if you've done your homework and found a car that is safe and reliable and meets all your needs, you could still make some mistakes. Be wary of high-tech gadgets and gizmos that cost more than they're worth and create their own set of problems. What are some of the worst offenders? Well, how about cruise control and electronic instrument readouts? Cruise control was hyped as the "must have" option a few years ago, but it's really useful only for motorists who use their vehicles for long periods of high-speed driving. Electronic instrument readouts are even worse because they can be difficult to read, particularly in direct sunlight.

When it comes to the outside of the car, buyers are often enticed by options like aluminum wheels, fog lights, sunroofs, tinted glass, and rooftop carriers. Aluminum wheels are standard on most sportscars, but they are often fragile and aren't always compatible with snow tires. Fog lights aren't necessary for most drivers and can annoy others on the road, and sunroofs are a great source of potential problems, from water leaks and rattles to wind-dust accumulation. Tinted glass actually jeopardizes your safety by reducing night vision, and it makes people – especially police officers – nervous. And rooftop carriers add to your car's wind-resistance, increasing fuel consumption by as much as 5 percent. You should purchase one of these only if your family does a lot of camping!

You also want to watch for "extras" that are supposed to keep your car looking good longer or are said to add to its fuel economy. Paint and fabric protectors and rustproofing are usually not necessary, for example. The former are just expensive "sealants" that do not work, and the latter has become nonessential because most automakers have extended their own rust warranties. You should definitely avoid gas-saving gadgets and fuel additives that attach to your fuel line or are poured into the fuel tank. According to North American consumer protection agencies, not one of these actually works to increase fuel efficiency. What's worse is that using them can render your car's warranty invalid!

Anything else to steer clear of? Well, how about ID etching and adjustable steering wheels? ID etching – which is supposed to be a theft-deterrent – can be quite expensive to buy from a dealer, and most communities offer the service for free periodically. An adjustable steering wheel is useful only if a vehicle is going to be driven regularly by more than one person. Even then, it can be dangerous if the adjustment interferes with airbag deployment.

Suspension systems that automatically provide a "hard" or "soft" ride are another unnecessary extra. Although it's favored by high-performance enthusiasts who want to feel every crack in the pavement, this option isn't much use unless you plan on carrying heavy loads and don't want the suspension to bottom out on you. Plus, it's expensive to repair. Side airbags have been shown to seriously injure car occupants who aren't positioned properly when they deploy. And satellite navigation systems – often promoted as the wave of the future – are simply an unnecessary distraction.

So now that you know a lot more about what makes a good car – and a bad one! – let's see what would be the best car for you and your family to buy. Remember, what's important is not the amount of money you spend. You'll get the best buy when you learn to separate the horsepower from the hype and the essential from the frivolous.

5

CAR OWNERSHIP:
MAKING THE GRADE

When cars were first introduced, they were seen simply as playthings for the very rich. In those days, the expectation was that buyers would pay cash on the spot to cover the entire purchase cost of the car. Everyone was accustomed to paying "cash on the barrelhead" for goods. Only special, once-in-a-lifetime items, such as pianos, could be bought on an installment plan. And even when the price for vehicles like Henry Ford's Model T began to drop dramatically, they were still beyond the reach of the average family.

In 1911, the Studebaker Company offered automobiles for purchase on a deferred-payment plan. Reluctantly, the rest of the car companies followed suit, and in less than ten years, 50 percent of all cars sold in America were being bought on time payments. Other businesses, seeing the powerful draw this was for consumers, also started selling their merchandise on installments, and we've been "buying on time" ever since! Perhaps that's a lucky thing, at the rate car prices are rising.

Today, with the North American economy vulnerable to the fluctuations of a global market and world events, savvy consumers are determined to reduce their debt load. They do not want to invest in high monthly payments for a car or minivan that's more than they need or costs far more than it's worth. At the same time, we all need vehicles that are safe, reliable, and capable of taking us where we need to go. That's why used cars, particularly those certified by manufacturers, are so popular. Buyers want reliability and comfort, but they don't want to burden themselves for years with a purchase that's guaranteed to lose more than half its value!

	Average Earnings	Price of a Model T
1912	$592	$600
1914	$627	$490
1916	$708	$360
1924	$1,303	$290

Buyer Beware

There's one foolproof way to ensure that you will get a terrific car – used or new – without taking on unrealistic payments or drowning in maintenance costs, and that is to *prepare*. You should invest at least one month of preparation time in your car-buying project. This includes at least two weeks for basic research and another two weeks to bargain with dealers to get the right car at the right price. If this seems like a big commitment, think about how much time you need to spend working on a science project to get an A. An A in car ownership

OH, THAT NEW CAR SMELL

There's something about the smell of a new car that is so attractive that they sell it in a can! But the truth is that the smell is a complex mixture of fabric and plastic components, adhesives, and sealers. Together, these are known as volatile organic compounds (VOCs). Gases from these materials make a diluted sea of VOCs that float about in the passenger compartment and create that "new car smell."

Commonly blamed for fogging window interiors, VOCs are now thought to be quite dangerous. A two-year study by Australia's Commonwealth Scientific and Industrial Research Organization (CSIRO), released in 2001, found that VOC emissions can impair driving ability in just a few minutes and may be responsible for many accidents. The study said that gases from vinyl and plastic materials in new cars can cause headaches, nausea, and drowsiness. The chemicals involved also include benzene – a known cancer-causing agent – which was found in at least one case to be at five times the recommended exposure level.

Your car purchase should involve three separate negotiations: one for the price of the car, one for the price of any add-ons, and one for the financing. Don't let the seller lump these three together.

requires a lot of reading and thinking about what you really need and how much you can afford to spend.

Smart buyers follow four golden rules: 1. they know their budget and stick to it; 2. they do their homework and haggle; 3. they time the market and remain flexible; and 4. they get the best price for their old vehicle.

Knowing your budget and sticking to it is rule number one because all too often low finance rates can make you buy more car than you need or can afford. Decide what you realistically require, set a target interest rate, and then stick to the decisions you've made.

Rule number two is to *do your homework*. Research vehicle costs on the Internet before you ever step into a showroom. (At the back of this book, you'll find a list of websites for some of the more reliable sources.) Once you've educated yourself about car prices and determined how big a monthly payment you can afford, you're ready to haggle. Don't be afraid to do this even when dealers say they have a "no haggle" policy. In most cases, this "policy" will be forgotten as soon as you head for the door. Some people even use fax machines to get dealers

TEN RULES FOR BUYING NEW

1. Never buy a vehicle during its first year on the market, just after an extensive redesign, or during a labor strike.
2. Choose a rebate over low-interest financing if you're buying a moderately priced vehicle.
3. Have several models in mind and look for cheaper versions sold by another division of the same automaker.
4. Make sure your contract states that a free loaner will be supplied whenever you need warranty repairs that take more than a day.
5. Ask the dealer for a specific delivery date and a "protected" price while you make your decision. If the price goes up while you're thinking things over, you will still be able to buy at the original rate.
6. Don't buy an extended warranty for vehicles with proven reliability.
7. Make sure you and the dealer use the same figures. You will move up from the dealer's wholesale price, while he'll try to move down from the manufacturer's suggested retail price.
8. Don't go to the showroom alone. Recruit a tough-minded friend or family member to go with you. Women – yes, your mom! – are particularly effective negotiators because they do sweat the details.
9. If you're leasing, watch out for hidden fees and a low mileage allowance (less than 15,000 miles [24,000 kilometers] per year). You should also avoid excess mileage costs of more than five cents a mile (ten cents a kilometer).
10. Keep the lease as short as possible (no more than three years) and ask for arbitration if the dealer alleges excessive wear and tear when the vehicle is returned.

HOW MUCH IS THAT CONVERTIBLE ONLINE?

A growing number of car sales are now being conducted online. When a car shopper fills out an online form through an Internet referral service, the information is forwarded to local affiliates, and they then will respond with price offers. Studies show that online consumers pay about 2 percent less for their cars than those who negotiate the traditional way. Critics of this process say that the benefits are really only for people who hate bargaining, but savvy economists note that Internet shopping does lower prices because the shopper is usually better informed. Plus, the referral services use their own power to make sure dealers keep prices low.

As your parents know, it's important that you establish and maintain a good credit rating. That way, a dealer can't refuse low-interest financing by claiming your credit is bad.

to bid against each other. Dealers who receive an "official" bid request are much more likely to bargain with you than if you simply walk into the dealership on your own or ask for prices over the phone.

The third rule is to *be patient and flexible*. Shop when sales are slow and you may find a 10 percent drop in the listed price. Also, always turn down fancy extras like window-etching, rust-proofing, and paint protection. As we saw in the last chapter, these extras are usually overpriced and won't add to your car's value. And watch out for "hidden" charges, especially transportation or freight charges to have the car delivered from the factory to your dealer, pre-delivery inspection fees (commonly referred to as PDI fees) that are more than 2 percent of the vehicle's cost, and all acquisition, disposal, and administrative fees.

The final rule is to *do as much research* on your old car as you do on the car you intend to buy. You will get more money for your trade-in by selling it privately, but it takes more time and can expose you to a lawsuit if the buyer brings the car back and claims you misrepresented the vehicle. If you do decide to trade in your car with the dealer you're going to buy from, don't talk about the value of your trade-in until you've settled on the price of the new car. This way, you won't be confused by the two sets of figures.

The Case for Buying Used

Most of the time, it really is a far better deal to buy a used car. The resale value of most new vehicles is reduced by 50 percent after just three years. In other words, a new car that sells for $30,000 will be worth only $15,000 after three years. But after an additional three years, that same car, sold used at $15,000, will be worth $10,000. Over time, the pace of depreciation slackens and the car will be viewed more for its functionality than its cachet.

Used cars are also "green" cars. They are recycled goods that don't require additional energy or resources to produce – and they don't add to traffic congestion. By repairing the vehicle, rather than replacing it, you are also maximizing the car's longevity, preserving your money along with the environment.

However, safety must be an important consideration when you're deciding whether to buy new or used. Most new cars earn impressive crashworthiness scores in tests sponsored by the government and insurance companies. Many older cars weren't built as well, though, and there can be other safety-related issues.

WHEN NEW IS USED

There is no guarantee that any new vehicle you decide to buy really is new. Unfortunately, odometer fraud is becoming more and more widespread. The odometer, which measures how many miles (or kilometers) the car has traveled, can quite easily be disconnected or tampered with. This is most common in new vehicles that tend to accumulate significant mileage in a short period, such as demonstrators or cars used by a dealer's sales staff. Also, it is estimated that 10 percent of new cars are damaged during transport and repaired by the dealer before being sold. Fortunately, if the dealer doesn't disclose this fact, the buyer can demand both a refund and punitive damages.

With used cars, it is always a good idea to have a trusted mechanic check the odometer for you before you buy. A trained eye can usually tell if a car's wear and tear is consistent with the odometer reading. No one should ever buy a used vehicle without checking the car thoroughly through an independent garage.

And don't forget to check the driver's doorjamb for the plate that gives the car's real birthday! Responsible dealers will also have checked the vehicle identification number (VIN) on the dash, which will tell them if the car has been wrecked or doesn't actually belong to the seller.

THE LAND WHERE CARS NEVER DIE!

If you think a six- or eight-year-old car seems ancient, imagine living in a country like Cuba, where owning an automobile is still considered a luxury. In that island nation, cars became stuck in a time warp in the late 1950s, when the Cuban revolution led to an American blockade and trade embargo. The only "new" cars permitted now are Russian, and many of the vehicles seen on the streets are forty to fifty years old.

When a Cuban car is finally no longer able to run, its parts are salvaged for use on other vehicles. Tires are so expensive that patches are now applied to patches! Since new parts are virtually impossible to obtain on the island, Cuban mechanics are known for their almost magical abilities to make repairs; some have even used the pistons of Soviet trucks in Chryslers from the 1950s. Not surprisingly, some of the world's strangest-looking cars can be seen on the streets of Havana.

Take airbags, for example. Depowered airbags – which are less dangerous for short-statured occupants – weren't phased into production until 1997. On the other hand, side-mounted airbags are now standard on many new cars, despite the fact that researchers say they can be deadly to passengers who are "improperly positioned." Whichever way you decide to go, used or new, be sure the car you're buying is safe and reliable.

Many people also think new cars are a better buy because they're more efficient and less expensive to maintain. But as odd as it may sound, new cars seldom achieve the fuel performance touted by carmakers. In fact, you can expect fuel efficiency to be 10 to 15 percent lower than it should be until the car has been "broken in." Used cars do require more maintenance than new vehicles that are still covered by the automaker's warranty. However, the repairs will cost about a third less if you have them done at independent garages, which pretty much wipes out a new car's maintenance advantage.

It's also quite common for new cars to emit a rotten-egg smell from the exhaust because the catalytic converter (an

It's getting pretty hard to find a vehicle that's more than ten years old and is still safe and reliable. As an alternative, many smart consumers look for "orphaned vehicles," models that have been axed because of waning popularity or because they didn't fit the automaker's long-term plans. Chevy's Sunbird and the Ford Probe are two good examples.

RECOMMENDED USED CARS: 1980S TO MID-1990S VEHICLES

Chrysler: All rear-drives and the Colt import
Ford: All rear-drives, Escort (1991 and later), and Probe
GM: All rear-drives, Astro, Caprice, Malibu, Montana, Roadmaster, Safari, and Venture
Honda: Accord, Civic, and Odyssey
Hyundai: Accent, Elantra, and Tiburon
Mazda: Miata, MX-3, MX-6, 929, and Precidia
Mercury: Grand Marquis and Villager
Nissan: Axxess, Quest, Sentra, and Stanza
Subaru: All front-drives, Justy, and post-1995 Forester, Impreza, and Legacy
Toyota: Avalon, Camry, Celica, Corolla, Sienna, and Supra

TEN RULES FOR BUYING USED

1. Try to buy a vehicle that's presently being used by someone in your family. You will have a good idea of how it was driven and maintained, and you can use the same garage that has been repairing the car for years.
2. If you're buying from a dealer, delay your purchase until mid-year, when clearance rebates on new cars bring a lot of inexpensive trade-ins on the market.
3. Look for high-mileage vehicles being sold by reputable rental agencies, like Budget. Budget sells its vehicles directly to the public, with honest money-back guarantees and reasonably priced extended warranties.
4. Refuse all preparation or "administration" charges.
5. Stay away from most American front-wheel drives. They fail more frequently and require costlier repairs.
6. Be wary of cheap, discontinued American models that were dropped because of poor quality (such as the Chrysler Omni/Horizon, the Ford Tempo/Topaz, and the GM Corsica/Beretta). You can check a model's past performance in reliable sources such as the Lemon-Aid guides.
7. Avoid European models. Parts and servicing can be a problem, and quality control is declining.
8. Look for five- to ten-year-old, one-owner Japanese models.
9. Shop for used rear-wheel-drive, full-sized wagons or vans, instead of American minivans. The American vehicles are not as reliable or as fuel-efficient as their Japanese counterparts.
10. Don't buy for fuel economy alone. A four-cylinder minivan is cheap to run, but highway merging will be a white-knuckle affair.

STANDING THE TEST OF TIME

In 2002, *Consumer Reports* surveyed the owners of nearly 480,000 1995 to 2002 model-year vehicles and ranked the cars for overall reliability. The magazine found that nine of the thirteen most reliable year 2000 makes were Asian; only two were from North American producers. The other two top-rated brands were European.

Consumer Reports says its survey discovered that among three-year-old cars, there were roughly 55 problems per every 100 vehicles. Many of the Japanese makes had half that number of defects, as shown in the chart below.

MAKE	PROBLEMS	MAKE	PROBLEMS	MAKE	PROBLEMS	MAKE	PROBLEMS
Acura	21	Mitsubishi	42	Plymouth	57	Saturn	70
Toyota	25	Lincoln	47	Dodge	59	GMC	72
Lexus	25	Buick	49	Audi	64	Mercedes-Benz	73
Honda	32	Hyundai	53	Oldsmobile	67	Volkswagen	74
Mazda	34	BMW	54	Pontiac	68	Cadillac	82
Subaru	36	Chrysler	56	Jeep	68		
Saab	37	Ford	56	Chevrolet	69		
Nissan	40	Mercury	57	Volvo	70		

emissions device attached to the exhaust pipe) won't function properly. Sometimes the smell lingers for more than a year. Perhaps it seems unfair to focus on this one, temporary problem, but when you've paid about $30,000 for your wheels and your passengers are wondering if you have serious digestion difficulties ... well, you get the picture!

The Costs of Car Ownership

Once you buy a car, whether it's new or used, keep in mind that you'll have to spend a fair bit of money each year maintaining it. Maintenance costs can be high, and these include not only repairs and routine upkeep but also fuel and oil, which fluctuate wildly in price. You'll also have to pay annual license and registration fees and insurance coverage, even if the car sits in the garage all year.

Buying cheap gas and keeping your driving to a minimum are the best ways to control fuel costs. Premium fuel is usually a waste of money, and it can foul up your emissions system.

But don't get complacent just because your car isn't driven much or doesn't have any problems – yet. In fact, non-use can make a vehicle deteriorate more quickly, because key components dry out and rust. The solution? Find a reliable independent garage and have the mechanic set up a maintenance schedule specific to your car and its eccentricities.

But what about your friendly dealer's service bay? Carmakers are more than happy to supply you with regular maintenance schedules, but can they really be trusted? Not according to a Canadian Broadcasting Corporation television show that exposed the inflated prices Mazda dealers were charging for periodic maintenance. Car dealers are known to grossly inflate the cost of this service, and sometimes they will even threaten to deny the warranty if maintenance isn't

BETTER SAFE THAN SORRY

No matter how well you care for your car, accidents and weather-related breakdowns can occur, so the following emergency supplies should be kept in every vehicle: bottled water, non-perishable food, a first-aid kit, flares, blankets, critical medication, a fire extinguisher, a flashlight and batteries, sanitation supplies (such as plastic bags, tissues, and moistened towelettes), basic tools (such as screwdrivers, pliers, and a knife), rope and plastic tape, comfortable shoes, and candles and matches. If you live in snow country, you should also have a window scraper, extra wiper fluid, spare wiper blades, a small folding shovel, a bag of salt or sand for traction, and an extra pair of boots.

But the best protection is prevention, and that means always keeping your gas tank half full in case of emergency and filling it up completely before setting out on a long trip. If a sudden storm or power blackout strands you on the highway or in traffic, the extra fuel will allow you to keep your car running so you can stay warm.

done in their shop. Unfortunately, this kind of intimidation and price-gouging is permitted by law.

No matter who you use to keep your car running as it should, periodic maintenance will help you avoid many potential problems. Just like ice skates that don't get sharpened, a good car can fail simply because of a lack of attention! One good way to maintain your car is to follow this basic checklist every time you go to the gas station for a fill-up:

1. Check the engine oil.
2. Check the transmission fluid.
3. Check the power-steering fluid.
4. Check the brake fluid.
5. Check the coolant.
6. Check the washer fluid.

Other basic maintenance routines include keeping your car clean, checking the lights, and making sure the tires have the correct air pressure.

With some careful planning, you will have a first car that's a dream, rather than a nightmare. Of course, cars, like computers, are changing all the time, and each month and year sees more styles, increased power, and greater comfort. Let's take a look now at what you can expect to see on the roads of the future.

6

CARS OF
TOMORROW – TODAY

There is no doubt about it – there *will* continue to be cars in our future. But they will be different, primarily because of alternative power sources and new safety features. They'll inevitably become safer and more environmentally friendly. These developments will be incremental, however, and most changes will not be immediately apparent. Outwardly, cars won't look all that unusual at first, but in twenty years, designers will have greater freedom and their creativity will fuel new fads.

Cars simply must change if they are to survive as our most common means of land transport. Automakers know they have to build cars that burn less fuel more cleanly, yet they have lobbied extensively to delay and dilute voluntary emissions standards, forcing governments to step in. Even in an industry that has generated such profound societal change, it is not always easy to shift gears.

But the reality is that the gasoline-fueled internal combustion engine is reaching its limits. Vehicles are still only 20 to 25 percent efficient in converting the energy content of fuels into drive–wheel power, and it is estimated that 30 percent is the maximum efficiency level. Meanwhile, the continued production of carbon dioxide remains a serious threat to our environment. So, with increasing commitment, the major auto manufacturers are finally turning their attention to producing dream machines that are also green machines.

But how do we put the genie back in the bottle? In 2003, for the first time in history, the average American household had more cars than drivers, according to a report from the U.S. Department of Transportation. And by 2020, according to projections, 15 percent of the world's people, double the current figure, will own a vehicle! Even with diminished fuel emissions, the impact of that many cars on the planet's climate will be devastating, especially when you consider that automobiles are now responsible for up to two-thirds of all urban smog and one-quarter of the carbon dioxide in our air.

Then there's the question of fuel supply. Automobiles were invented shortly after the discovery of huge oil fields in the United States and other countries. At the time, the oil supply seemed endless. But production is already slowing down, and oil-rich countries are using the resource as a political weapon, which could make reliable supplies a problem in the future. And even if the supply was more reliable, with the

Emissions standards are limits set by a governing body to regulate the amount of air pollutants that get emitted from a vehicle's tailpipe or leak out of its engine.

TOO MANY CARS!

Pollution concerns, fuel limitations, and traffic gridlock should suggest that alternatives to personal car ownership, such as public transit and community-based shared car ownership, are the way of the future. However, the automobile industry shows no sign of slowing down. China, the world's most populous country, is now on the road to becoming a car culture. Its annual car sales topped the one-million mark in 2002, and increased demand from the country's growing middle class and the availability of cheaper models will continue to spur sales on. With lower production costs attracting plants from industry giants such as Honda and General Motors, China is expected to lead the world in volume growth over the next decade or so and shortly move into third spot (behind the U.S. and Japan)!

With only 5 percent of the world's population, Canada and the United States together emit 24 percent of the world's carbon dioxide. On a per capita level, North Americans are responsible for emitting nearly twenty tons (more than 20,000 kilograms) of climate-changing carbon dioxide per year, a figure that dwarfs that of other regions of the world.

dramatic increase in sales expected in emerging markets such as China, Brazil, India, and Russia, there's simply not going to be enough oil available to fuel cars in the traditional way.

The Search for Alternative Fuel Sources

Although some experts argue that making our cars go farther on a gallon of gas is the biggest single step we can take toward cutting our crippling dependence on oil and curbing global warming, the auto industry recognizes that viable options to traditional fuel sources must be developed if cars are to remain part of our everyday lives. "Green cars" – that is, cars that are environmentally friendly, yet still efficient and fun to drive – are critical to the future of auto manufacturing.

As the industry struggles to adapt to the reality that the gasoline era is coming to an end, manufacturers like Honda and Toyota have taken the lead in developing functional hybrid models that are gaining popularity. Several initially reluctant American-based carmakers have now joined in. Everyone recognizes that a race to renew the industry through a new core technology has begun, and the major players understand that sitting on the sidelines is risky. Every manufacturer wants to develop the world's next "people's car."

Hybrid Cars

A hybrid car is one that uses some combination of a conventional gasoline engine and an electric motor. The hybrid's battery is recharged by the internal combustion engine and by energy collected when the car brakes. The battery powers an electric motor that either adds to or takes over for the gasoline-powered engine. In some hybrid models, the electric motor assists when the car is climbing hills or accelerating sharply. In others, the electric motor takes over at low speeds. In all hybrids, the gas engine shuts off when the car stops. This extremely efficient combination means that hybrid cars produce nearly no toxic emissions and can achieve significant fuel savings. They could be considered "transition age" cars, as they are filling the gap until viable alternative fuels are found. And while they are still more expensive then traditional vehicles,

Hybrid vehicles have been in existence for quite some time. Diesel–electric buses, for example, can run from the power they derive from overhead wires or from diesel fuel alone. A motorized pedal bike, or moped, is also a kind of hybrid, in that it uses both the power of an engine and the power produced by the pedal-pushing rider.

incentives such as tax credits are encouraging buyers and prices are expected to fall slowly.

Hydrogen Fuel: Driving the Future?

Hydrogen is the fuel that sends spaceships to the moon, and it produces no climate-altering pollution. It also has another important advantage over other fuels: it is the most plentiful element in the universe. If we switched to a so-called hydrogen economy, no one country would have control over the production and distribution of the world's power.

Currently, the governments of the European Union, the United States, Canada, and Japan are investing huge amounts of research money into addressing the difficulties of harnessing such a tremendous source of fuel. Basic questions such as

HOW DO HYDROGEN FUEL CELLS WORK?

The fuel cell creates an electric current through a chemical reaction, but unlike a regular battery, it doesn't wear out or need to be recharged. Fuel cells are non-polluting because they emit only heat and water as by-products.

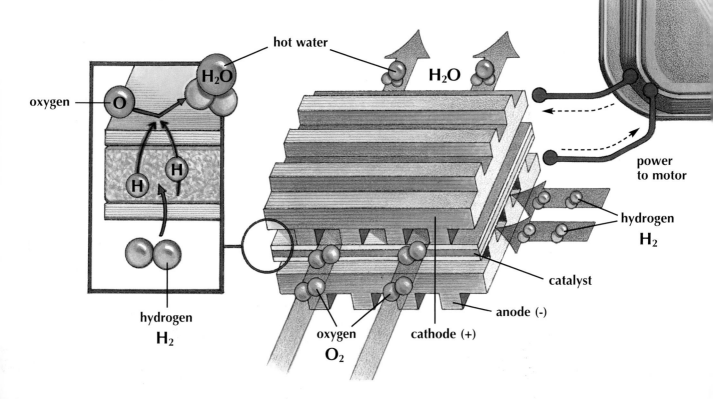

Everyone has read about the horrific 1937 fire that destroyed the famous Hindenburg zeppelin, the hydrogen-filled craft that was at the forefront of transatlantic air service. For decades, the word "hydrogen" has evoked memories of the unforgettable newsreel footage of the disaster. But recent investigations have found that production flaws in the zeppelin's fabric covering were to blame for the tragedy. Such findings are welcome proof that hydrogen is a fuel that is just as safe as gasoline.

how best to store and distribute hydrogen in its natural gaseous state are complicating the process of introducing it as a major fuel source. Nevertheless, the idea of converting to a hydrogen economy is gaining favor, since such an economy would rely heavily on the pipelines, storage facilities, and fuel stations that are already used to produce and deliver oil and gas.

The shift to hydrogen as our principal source of power would likely create a revolution in the entire world economy. Hydrogen fuel cell technology has been described as "the power train of the future," and the world's automakers are already putting prototypes of hydrogen-powered cars in their showrooms.

Meanwhile, American car giants are working to develop fuel cell stacks, fuel processors, electrolyzers, and the systems around them into products for both stationary and transportable uses. Just as James Watt did with steam power, researchers hope to turn fuel cells into a power source that can be harnessed to make high-volume, highly durable, affordable products. Now that the shortcomings of the first battery-powered cars have been laid to rest by hybrid cars that never need plugging in, no one is laughing at the prospect of an "ever-ready" car with enough energy to outlast any skeptic.

But don't get too excited just yet. Although the big auto manufacturers are collaborating in order to accelerate progress, hydrogen-powered cars won't be rolling off the assembly line for mass-market distribution for another ten or twenty years, which means we still have to address the immediate problem of declining fuel efficiency in our current gas-guzzlers. In fact, some experts believe the future lies not with fuels cells and hybrids at all but with improved emissions output and the increased use of other alternative fuels.

Natural Gas and Diesel Fuel

Fuel systems for cars powered by natural gas, a cleaner-burning fuel, and propane, a liquid fuel extracted primarily from natural gas, are being developed in the United States to meet tough emissions standards for large vehicles such as forklifts and Zamboni machines. In Canada, with the dearth of public refueling stations for cars powered by natural gas, home-fueling systems that can hook into residential gas lines are being sold by private companies. In fact, it is widely believed that home refueling will help to increase consumer acceptance of natural gas for vehicles. Imagine fueling your car at home!

Others champion the engine that is used by almost half the new cars in Europe. It uses diesel fuel and is inherently more fuel-efficient than internal combustion engines. The automobile and oil industries in America are cool to diesel power, however, leaving the field almost completely to European auto manufacturers like Mercedes-Benz and Volkswagen.

Crop-based Fuels

Believe it or not, Rudolf Diesel used simple vegetable oil to power his first engine at the 1900 Paris World's Fair. The idea of a crop-based fuel has recently been "rediscovered" by a sizable number of diesel enthusiasts. In 1998, the U.S. National Renewable Energy Laboratory released a study on a fuel called biodiesel, which is essentially vegetable oil with methanol and lye. Biodiesel results in fewer harmful emissions than petroleum-based diesel and costs no more.

The price of vegetable oil is beginning to come down as well, thanks to the growing demand for soy protein in food (if you grind soybeans, you'll be left with 80 percent soy meal and 20 percent oil). And that's not all. Restaurateurs normally have to pay someone to haul off the gallons of vegetable oil used each day in their fryers. This oil traditionally gets dumped in a landfill or perhaps used in animal feed. But if all of that wasted oil is salvaged and filtered, it can be added to any standard diesel engine that has been outfitted with a special conversion kit. Conversion kits have been installed in a variety of diesel vehicles – Volkswagen TDIs, tractors, large Dodge four-by-fours, and even a used Greyhound bus. From there, the only detectable difference will be the faint odor of french fries and a noticeable lack of diesel fumes. The change in odor is not the only benefit, however. Emissions are reduced significantly.

Another alternative fuel is ethanol, which is made from sugar cane. In the mid-1980s, Brazil had brief success with its

WHAT'S COOKING?

In 2002, it was reported that a Welsh police team called the Frying Squad was sniffing out motorists who were fueling their cars with used cooking oil. In one small community, residents were using a homemade mixture of methanol and cooking oil in diesel-powered cars to avoid high fuel prices. So what's the problem? Well, traditional fuel is a great source of tax revenue, and in many countries, it is a crime to circumvent the system to avoid paying those taxes. In Wales, offenders usually give themselves away because the cars they drive emit the distinctive odor of french fry grease.

sugar producers, who were eager to support the country's scheme to avoid the high costs of imported energy after the world oil shortages of the 1970s. At one point, three-quarters of all new cars sold in Brazil ran on pure ethanol. Unfortunately, a subsequent surge in the world price of sugar discouraged producers from selling it to local distilleries, since they could earn more by exporting it. However, with oil prices on the rise again, Brazil may once more provide the rest of the world with a plausible alternative fuel source.

Other sources of biodiesel fuel, such as animal fats, are also being developed. The idea is to blend these fuels with regular petroleum diesel at the pumps. Ethanol, for example, can be put into gasoline in a 10 percent blend. Cars can actually run on a blend that is as much as 85 percent ethanol if their fuel- and air-intake mechanisms are adjusted.

Solar Power

Not too long ago, the answer to our pollution concerns seemed to lie in using energy from the sun to charge a large battery to power a car engine. Solar power is created when sunlight strikes specially designed panels and, through a process called photovoltaic conversion, is changed into electricity. Unfortunately, most people believe solar power does not have quite the same potential for success as hydrogen fuel cells. Some skeptics think this is because solar power is virtually free. Until automakers and oil magnates succeed in owning the sun, they charge, research into solar power will be conducted only by universities and other non-profit organizations. The reality, however, is that the technology needed to do the conversion is still too expensive; a solar panel for one solar-powered car can cost hundreds of thousands of dollars to produce. But some industry watchers remain hopeful that one day there will be a mass-produced hybrid car that has batteries charged partially by the sun.

Smart Cars?

Fuel alternatives are not the only changes that are associated with cars of the future. So-called smart car technology is already stumping parking lot attendants and valets around the world! One new car requires a cardlike plastic device to be inserted before it will start. Another has a start button that simulates the starter of a professional racing car. Remote starters that allow drivers to pre-heat or pre-cool their cars

FLYING CARS?

Thanks to the availability of new lightweight materials, advances in computer modeling, and the advent of computer-controlled aircraft, the "space utility vehicle" is no longer a fantasy. In fact, it is very close to becoming reality. There are approximately eighty patents on file at the United States Patent and Trademark Office for various kinds of flying cars, some which have even worked! If mass-production becomes possible, they could be the answer to our ever-worsening traffic problems. But if you think the rules of the road are complicated now, imagine the sorts of directional signs and "traffic" regulations that would be required to manage cars that fly!

while they are still inside the house are becoming commonplace. And some new cars have computerized controls that are so futuristically designed that their operating systems look like the control deck of the NASA space center!

Most of the technological developments in car design today are geared toward safety. New safety innovations range from ceiling-mounted cameras that allow you to keep an eye on what's going on in the back seat to sensors that can detect a car in your blind spot and flash strategically positioned lights in the roof pillars to alert you. There could even be a rear-view camera, cameras built into the outside mirrors, and a big screen in the console in place of the usual array of dials and buttons. But too many neat gadgets can leave consumers cold – not to mention confused!

To solve modern-day traffic woes, designers are introducing driver-assistance systems that will make cars safer and also help traffic flow more smoothly. Some units will sound an alarm if you start to doze off; others will track the speed and location of the vehicle directly ahead, warning you when you are getting too close. Not only could driver-assist systems prevent crashes when drivers attempt to change lanes, but they might also reduce the number of times cars must quickly brake, helping to prevent traffic jams. The fewer times any one driver hits the brakes, the theory goes, the smoother everyone's commute will be.

FLOATING CARS

Amphibious vehicles were first mass-produced in 1961, when the German-built Amphicar came to North American shores – literally! Equipped with a powerful British-built Triumph engine in the rear, the Amphicar had a top speed of seventy miles (112 kilometers) an hour on land and seven miles (11 kilometers) an hour on water. In the water, the front wheels acted as rudders.

Unfortunately, American federal emissions and safety standards spelled the end of the Amphicar in late 1967. But the dream didn't die. Today, James Bond wannabes (who have recently won the lottery) can buy the jet-propelled Aquada, which zips along at a very respectable one hundred miles (160 kilometers) an hour on land and thirty miles (48 kilometers) an hour on water.

The Black Box

These data recorders, the size of a VCR tape, are just like similar devices found in airplanes. They have been hidden under the seats or in the center consoles of millions of Ford and GM cars and trucks since the early 1990s. Experts say that highway safety could be vastly improved if black boxes were installed in all cars to record information about crashes. Enthusiastically promoted by government and law enforcement agencies around the world, these data recorders have had a positive effect on accident prevention: European studies show that drivers who know their vehicles are equipped with the device have an accident rate 20 to 30 percent below average and drive more slowly.

So Many Cars, So Little Road

With the increase in personal car ownership and the lack of enthusiasm for public transit, traffic congestion on our roads is increasing. Gridlock is now reaching frightening proportions in most heavily populated areas. Our roads were not meant to handle such a high volume of traffic, and the density of cars in our major cities is reaching ridiculous levels. Hydraulic lifts are even being built to allow for car-stacking systems in downtown parking garages. The situation is so bad that in some parts of the world, a "congestion" charge is levied to regulate traffic. In Rome, Italy, city officials charge vehicles each time they enter zones that are gridlocked to the point of paralysis at certain

THE DARK HORSE OF A GREEN FUTURE?

This Japanese-made "toy car," produced by the Takara toy company, is powered by tiny motors mounted on the rear wheels. The single-seater electric Q-Car runs for about fifty miles (80 kilometers) before its battery needs recharging.

Battery-operated automotive technology continues to improve in anticipation of advances in hydrogen fuel cell technology. With fuel cell vehicles and so-called hybrids getting most of the attention – and sales – so far, no one has come up with a battery that is inexpensive enough to offset the frequent recharging needed. So while the Japanese government has set a goal of having fifty thousand fuel cell cars on the roads by 2010, and five million by 2020, no such mandate exists for electrics. However, drivers of battery-electric cars are crazy about them and believe that the "plug it in and go" capability of vehicles like the Q-Car makes them easier to support. Indeed, some power companies in Japan are already starting to build dedicated recharging stations for electric cars.

times of the day. This system has been so successful that other large metropolises, such as London, England, have introduced similar schemes. It is now generally agreed that building more roads and widening existing ones are not forward-thinking solutions to the problem of traffic congestion.

"Are We There Yet?"

The automobile industry continues to dither about developing cars that will satisfy the demands of the environmentally responsible. So what can you do to ensure that the car you drive in 2020 will reflect revolutionary changes in the industry?

First of all, you can start asking a lot of questions about the cars your friends and family members drive. For example, despite the popularity of SUVs, these four-wheel-drive gas-guzzlers receive failing grades in almost every area that counts, including safety. Their fuel economy is atrocious, and most are sold to individuals or families who have no real practical reason for driving one. "Carmakers seem to have an instinct for putting their marketing and design talents into anything but addressing their products' harm to the planet," says John DeCicco, author of a 2002 report issued by the nonprofit Environmental Defense organization.

If greener cars are to be put on the road, they must be not only affordable but easy to start, easy to run, and easy to refuel. Until demand increases, however, green alternatives will be more costly to manufacture. Car companies won't change until consumers force them to change, and the best way for us to do that is to be well informed and demand technologies that will have a positive impact on the environment around us.

In 1944, E. B. White, the author of *Charlotte's Web*, observed that "everything in life is somewhere else, and you can get there in a car." Our cars provide us with a key to the world – friends, family, fun, and future. The automobile industry must be encouraged to support innovative designs and fuel technologies so that the world of tomorrow will be full of "somewhere elses" that we all want to get to in a car!

WHERE TO LOOK

You can find a lot of information about cars on the Internet. But you do have to be sure that what you find is truthful. To separate online fact from fiction, follow the 5 Ws of online research!

1. Who is the source of the information?
- Find the website's author(s) by looking at the site's contact information.
- Check out the author and/or organization by typing the name(s) into a search engine and seeing what else comes up.
- Use those other sites to confirm that the organization or author is a credible, authoritative source of information.

2. What are you getting?
- Does the site clearly state its goals and purpose?
- Does the site offer more than one viewpoint, or at least give links to sites with different perspectives?
- Does the site guide you to other resources?
- Does the site seem biased? For instance, does it rely on sweeping, unsubstantiated statements?

3. When was the site created or last updated?
- Look for the date when the material was posted online.
- Make sure that any links to other sites still work.

4. Where does this site come from?
- Learn the meaning of the various components of a site's address, its uniform resource locator (URL). This can give you useful clues about its source.

5. Why are you here?
- Is the Internet the best place to go for the information you need?
- Will you be able to verify the information you find?

More information on evaluating Internet sources can be found on the website of the Media Awareness Network (www.media-awareness.ca).

SITES TO SEARCH

Alberta Vehicle Cost Calculator (www1.agric.gov.ab.ca/app24/costcalculators/vehicle/getvechimpls.jsp)
Compare the ownership and operating costs of vehicles by plugging in variations in purchase price, options, fuel type, interest rates, or length of ownership.

ALLDATA Service Bulletins (www.alldata.com/consumer/TSB/yr.html)
Free summaries of automotive recalls and technical service bulletins.

American Automobile Association (www.aaa.com)

The Auto Channel (www.theautochannel.com)
A multimedia resource site with excellent information to help you choose a new or used vehicle. Updated daily.

Autopedia (www.autopedia.com)
An online automotive encyclopedia that's easy to use, this site includes complete coverage of all the lemon law statutes in the United States.

BBC-TV's Top Gear Car Reviews (www.topgear.beeb.com)
Top Gear blows the whistle on the best and worst European vehicles, auto products, and industry practices.

Canadian Automobile Association (www.caa.ca)

Canadian Driver (www.canadiandriver.com)
An exceptionally well-structured and current Canadian website for new- and used-vehicle reviews and consumer reports.

Carfax (www.carfax.com)
Use Carfax to see if a vehicle has been "scrapped," had flood damage, had its mileage turned back, or is stolen.

Cartrackers (www.cartrackers.com)
Used cars, consumer advice, and environmental issues are all covered on this site, which features a terrific image gallery and an excellent automotive glossary.

CBC-TV Marketplace (www.cbc.ca/consumers/market/)
An impressive array of automotive consumer information drawn from investigative reports and other sources.

Center for Auto Safety (www.autosafety.org)
A Ralph Nader–founded agency that provides free information about safety- and performance-related defects on all model vehicles.

Consumer Reports and Consumers Union (www.consumerreports.org)
CR's database is chock full of comparison tests and in-depth stories on products and services. The site includes a "Cars for Teens" special feature. You can also read *Consumer Reports* at your public library.

Crashtest.com (www.crashtest.com/netindex.htm)
A website where test results from around the world can be analyzed and compared.

Edmunds and Kelley Blue Book (www.edmunds.com and www.kbb.com)
These sites include in-depth reviews and owner critiques of almost every vehicle sold in North America, plus an informative readers' forum.

Ford Insider Info
(www.blueovalnews.com)
This website is the place to go for all the latest insider information on Ford's future models.

How Stuff Works
(auto.howstuffworks.com)
A site that makes the complicated simple, with plenty of easy-to-follow illustrations.

J. D. Power Consumer Centre: Automotive Ratings
(www.jdpower.com/cc/auto/index.jsp)
This site includes consumer ratings on vehicles and auto insurance providers.

Lemon-Aid
(www.lemonaidcars.com)
The official website of the Lemon-Aid annual consumer car guides.

National Highway Traffic Safety Administration
(www.nhtsa.dot.gov)
This American site has a comprehensive, free database covering owner complaints, recall campaigns, crashworthiness and rollover ratings, defect investigations, service bulletin summaries, and safety research papers.

The Roadhog Info Trough (www.w-rabbit.com/fote/index.html)
This Friends of the Earth website shows why SUV ownership is bad for the environment.

BOOKS TO READ

Adler, Dennis. *The Art of the Automobile: The 100 Greatest Cars* (New York: HarperResource, 2000).

Dinkel, John. *Road & Track Illustrated Automotive Dictionary* (Cambridge, MA : Bentley Publishers, 2000).

Edmonston, Phil. *Phil Edmonston's Lemon-Aid New Driver's Guide* (Toronto: Penguin, 2004).

Eyewitness Visual Dictionaries. *The Visual Dictionary of Cars* (Toronto: Stoddart, 1992).

Harrison, Peter. *Cars: A Young Person's Guide to Motoring History and How Cars Work* (Vancouver: Raincoast Books, 2001).

Morton, Desmond. *Wheels: The Car in Canada* (Toronto: Umbrella Press, 1998).

Weitzman, David. *Model T: How Henry Ford Built a Legend* (New York: Crown Publishers, 2002).

Willson, Quentin. *Cars: A Celebration* (London: Dorling Kindersley, 2001).

PLACES TO VISIT

Automotive Hall of Fame
21400 Oakwood Boulevard
Dearborn, Michigan 48124
www.automotivehalloffame.org

Canadian Automotive Museum
99 Simcoe Street South
Oshawa, Ontario L1H 4G7
www.oshawa.ca/tourism/can_mus2.asp

Henry Ford Museum
20900 Oakwood Boulevard
Dearborn, Michigan 48124-4088
www.hfmgv.org

Indianapolis Motor Speedway Hall of Fame
4790 W. 16th Street
Indianapolis, Indiana 46222
www.automuseum.com/INDYmuse.html

National Automobile Museum
10 Lake Street South
Reno, Nevada 89501
www.automuseum.org

Petersen Automotive Museum
6060 Wilshire Boulevard
Los Angeles, California 90036
www.petersen.org

Smithsonian Institution
1000 Jefferson Drive SW
Washington, D.C. 20560
www.si.edu/resource/faq/nmah/transportation.htm

GLOSSARY

Airbag
A large pillow or balloon that is deflated and stored in the steering wheel hub, the instrument panel, or some other interior surface of a vehicle. It is designed to form an air cushion that will restrain occupants in a collision.

Anti-lock braking system (ABS)
ABS keeps the wheels from locking up during braking and helps drivers maintain steering control on slippery surfaces. Its safety benefits are in dispute.

Brake shoe
An arc-shaped carrier to which the brake lining is mounted in a drum brake. Drum braking systems use a metal drum mounted on a wheel to form the outer shell of a brake. The brake shoes press against the drum to slow or stop wheel rotation. Disc brakes are considered more effective.

Caliper
This part of a disc brake holds the brake pads and straddles the disc. When the driver steps on the brake, the pads press against the disc to stop or slow the vehicle.

Clutch
This device connects or disconnects the parts of a transmission to produce different gear ratios. In an automatic transmission, the clutch is engaged and disengaged automatically as the gears change; in a standard car, the driver must manually engage or disengage the clutch as he or she shifts gears. In effect, the clutch transmits engine power to the wheels.

Computer-aided design (CAD)
CAD software is used to generate drawings and to perform complex design scenarios and structural analyses.

Damper
A hydraulic device similar to a shock absorber, the damper is attached to the steering linkage and helps minimize road shock and steering kickback.

Differential
This is what allows the right and left wheels to rotate at different speeds. When a car goes around a curve, the outside wheel must turn faster than the inside wheel to keep up.

Driveline
The driveline is all the parts of a vehicle's powertrain that lie between the transmission and the differential, including hubs, interconnecting shafts, gears, and clutches that transmit engine power to the wheels. The driveline, engine, and transmission combine to form the powertrain, or drivetrain.

Driveshaft
A shaft that rotates to transfer power from the transmission to the rear wheels.

Firewall
This wall isolates the engine compartment from the front cabin, which will stop engine fires from destroying the entire car.

Fuel injector
This delivers measured amounts of fuel directly into the intake valves of the cylinders of the internal combustion engine. It is more effective than a carburetor in determining the correct balance of fuel and air, which increases engine efficiency and reduces emissions.

Hydraulics
All hydraulic machines operate by transmitting force from one point to another using an incompressible fluid, usually oil. Because the fluid cannot be compressed, it is a very efficient way to transfer force. The most common use of hydraulics in your car is in the braking system. Hydraulic brakes use pistons or rotors in liquid-filled chambers to stop cars quickly and efficiently.

Ignition
This refers to any system that ignites a fuel-and-air mixture to create power in an engine. Most cars use a spark ignition system, with a spark plug setting fire to the mix of fuel and air. Diesel engines use compression ignition, igniting the mixture by compression force, rather than with a spark.

Spark plug
This is a screwed-in device that sits in the cylinder head of an internal combustion engine and emits a spark that ignites the cylinder's fuel-and-air mixture, providing power to the engine.

Starter
This is a device that sets an engine in motion. The starter converts electricity to mechanical energy by providing the spark that ignites the fuel. Diesel engines use a glow plug instead spark plugs.

Torque
Torque is a measure of how much an object will rotate when a specific force is exerted on it. The object rotates about an axis, or a pivot point. The farther the force is applied from the pivot point, the greater the torque will be. An example would be using a wrench to loosen a stubborn bolt. When you use a long wrench, you'll find you need to exert less force to turn the bolt. A shorter wrench would require more force. The same principle is at work in cars, where torque is used to turn the wheels and thus propel the car forward.

INDEX

Numbers in italics refer to illustrations.

alternative fuel sources, 63–68, *64*
American Automobile
  Association, 8
amphibious vehicles, 70
anti-lock brakes (ABS), 23
assembly lines, 9, 11
auto-starter, 16

Benz, Karl, 2, 8
bicycle makers, 8–9
Big Three automakers, 12
biodiesel fuel, 66, 67
black box recorders, 70
BMW, 26
braking system, 21, *21*
Bricklin SV-1, 29–30, *29*
Bricklin, Malcolm, 29
Bureau of Public Roads, 8

Canadian Automobile
  Association, 8
Canadian Broadcasting
  Corporation, 59
catalytic converter, 56, 58
chassis, 22
computer-aided design
  (CAD), 27–28
concept cars, 33, 34, *34*
Consumer Reports, 37, 38, 45, 58
cooling system, 23, *23*, 24
crankshaft, 3, 16, *16*
crashworthiness, 39, 41, 42, 54
crop-based fuels, 66–67
crossover cars, 34, 36
Cuba, 55
Cugnot, Nicolas, 2
Curved Dash Olds, 11, *11*

Daimler, Gottlieb, 6, *7*–8, 35
deferred payment plan, 49
DeLorean, 30, *30*, 32
DeLorean, John, 30, *30*
De Rivaz, Isaac, 5
diesel engine, 6
diesel fuel, 63, 66

Diesel, Rudolf, 6, 66
Dodrill-GMR Heart Machine, 28
driver-assistance systems, 69
Duryea, Charles, 8–9
Duryea, Frank, 8–9

Earle, Harley, 32, 33
Edgar, Graham, 20
electrical system, 17
emergency supplies, 59
emissions standards, 62
engines, 13–18
Environmental Defense
  organization, 72

Farmers' Anti-Automobile
  Society, 9
Federal Highway Administration, 8
flying cars, 69
Ford GT40, 33
Ford, Henry, 9–12, 35, 49
fuel economy conversion chart, 45

green cars, 54, 63
gridlock, 62, 70

Honda, Soichiro, 35
horsepower, 4, 18
hybrid cars, 18, 63–64
hydrogen fuel, 64–65
hydrogen fuel cell, 64, *64*, 65

internal combustion engine,
  5–8, 16–18, *17*
Isetta, 26, *26*

Kettering, Charles, 16

lemon, 38
Lemon-Aid car guides, 38, 57
Lenoir, Jean Joseph Etienne, 5–6
Leonardo da Vinci, 1, *1*

Maybach, William, 7
Mercedes, 35
Mini Cooper, 26
Model T, 11–12, 25, 49, *49*, 50
Morris, William Richard, 35

NASCAR Winston Cup, 28
natural gas, 65–66
Newton, Isaac, 1

octane rating system, 20
Olds, Ransom Eli, 9–10
orphaned vehicles, 56
Otto, Nicolaus, 6, 7, *7*, 16

Panhard et Levassor, 8
Papin, Denis, 2
patents, 5
people's car, 12, 63

Q-Car, 71, *71*

Rivolta, Renzo, 26

safety defects, 43
safety performance, 42
smart cars, 68–69
solar power, 67–68
steam engines, 3, *4*, 5
steam power, 2, *2*, 5
steering system, 20–21, *20*
Studebaker Company, 49
suspension system, 22, 48

Tin Lizzie, 11–12
tires, 22, 44, *44*
toy car, 71
Toyoda, Sakichi, 35
transmission system, 19–20, *19*

V8 engine, 18, *18*
vehicle identification number
  (VIN), 54
volatile organic compound
  (VOC), 50

Watt, James, 3, 4, 5
wheel, 3
White, E. B., 72
World Automotive Design
  Competition, 27